Everyman's Poetry

Everyman, I will go with thee,
and be thy guide

Thomas Hardy

Selected and edited by NORMAN PAGE

University of Nottingham

EVERYMAN

J. M. Dent · London

This edition first published by Everyman Paperbacks in 1998
Selection, Introduction and other critical apparatus
© J. M. Dent 1998

J. M. Dent
Orion Publishing Group
Orion House
5 Upper St Martin's Lane
London WC2H 9EA

Typeset by Deltatype Ltd, Birkenhead, Merseyside
Printed in Great Britain by
The Guernsey Press Co. Ltd, Guernsey, C. I.

British Library Cataloguing-in-Publication
Data is available on request

ISBN 0 460 87956 1

Contents

Note on the Author and Editor

THOMAS HARDY was born on 2 June 1840 in Higher Bockhampton, near Dorchester, in a cottage built by his grandfather. His father was a stonemason and master builder; his mother Jemima had been a domestic servant before her marriage. He left school at sixteen to be apprenticed to a Dorchester architect, and in 1862 moved to London to follow the same career. There he continued an arduous course of self-education and tried unsuccessfully to get his poems published. After returning to Dorset in 1867 he began to write fiction and between 1871 and 1897 published fourteen 'Wessex Novels' as well as about forty short stories. In 1874 he married Emma Lavinia Gifford, whom he had met in Cornwall in 1870; by the time of his marriage the success of his writings had enabled him to give up his architectural career. For more than ten years the couple lived in rented houses and flats in Dorset and London, but in 1885 they settled at Max Gate, built to Hardy's own designs on the outskirts of Dorchester and not far from his old home, and there he lived for the rest of his life.

Hardy began to publish collections of his verse only after giving up fiction, and *Wessex Poems* (1898, with Hardy's own illustrations) was followed by seven other volumes, the last of them (*Winter Words*, 1928) published posthumously. Emma's death in 1912 inspired some of his finest poems. In his later years Hardy was the most famous man of letters in England. After declining a knighthood, he was awarded the Order of Merit by King George V in 1910. He died on 11 January 1928. In his later years he wrote an autobiography, published (with some additions) soon after his death in the guise of a biography under the name of his second wife, Florence Emily Hardy, whom he had married in 1914.

NORMAN PAGE has lectured on Hardy in many parts of the world. His books include *Thomas Hardy* (1977) as well as editions of Hardy's *The Woodlanders* (Everyman), *The Well-Beloved* (Everyman), *The Mayor of Casterbridge* (Broadview Press) and *Jude the Obscure* (Norton). He has been editor of the *Thomas Hardy Annual* and the *Thomas Hardy Journal* and is a Vice-President of the Thomas Hardy Society. He is currently working on *The Oxford Reader's Companion to Thomas Hardy*.

Chronology of Hardy's Life

Year	Age	Life
1840		Hardy is born 2 June at Higher Bockhampton in the cottage built by his grandfather
1841		Birth of his sister, Mary
1848	8	Attends village school
1849–56	9–16	Attends school in Dorchester
1856	16	Articled to John Hicks, a Dorchester architect
1858	18	About now writes his first surviving poem, 'Domicilium'

Chronology of his Times

Year	Literary Context	Historical Events
1840		Great Irish famine; Penny Post is introduced
1842		Chartist riots
1846		Repeal of Corn Laws; Irish potato famine
1847	Charlotte Brontë, *Jane Eyre* Emily Brontë, *Wuthering Heights*	Railway reaches Dorchester
1848	Dickens, *Dombey & Son* Thackeray, *Vanity Fair* Pre-Raphaelite Brotherhood active	
1849	Ruskin *Seven Lamps of Architecture*	
1850	Death of Wordsworth Tennyson becomes Poet Laureate	
1851		The Great Exhibition in London
1853	Arnold, *Poems*	1853–6 The Crimean War
1855	Browning, *Men and Women* Elizabeth Gaskell, *North and South*	
1858	George Eliot, *Scenes of Clerical Life*	
1859	Darwin, *The Origin of Species*	
1860	Collins, *The Woman in White*	

Year	Age	Life
1862–7	22–7	Living in London, working as an architect, writes poetry but fails to get it published
1860s		Throughout this decade Hardy steadily loses his religious faith
1865	25	A short fictional piece called 'How I Built Myself a House' is published
1867	27	Returns to Dorset, begins his first novel, *The Poor Man and the Lady*
1868	28	Romantic affair with his cousin, Tryphena Sparks. *The Poor Man and the Lady* is rejected by publishers
1869	29	Works in Weymouth for an architect
1870	30	Meets and falls in love with Emma Lavinia Gifford while at St Juliot in Cornwall planning the restoration of the church
1871	31	*Desperate Remedies*, published anonymously, is a commercial failure
1872	32	Has minor success with *Under the Greenwood Tree*
1873	33	*A Pair of Blue Eyes*, Hardy's first novel to appear as a serial. Becomes a full-time novelist
1874	34	*Far from the Madding Crowd*, his first real success. Marries Emma Gifford. For next nine years they move from one lodging to another
1878	38	*The Return of the Native*. Becomes member of London's Savile Club

Year	Literary Context	Historical Events
1861	Palgrave's anthology, *The Golden Treasury* Hymns Ancient and Modern	American Civil War
1863	Death of Thackeray Mill, *Utilitarianism*	
1864	Newman, *Apologia pro Vita Sua*	
1865	Death of Elizabeth Gaskell	
1866	Swinburne, *Poems and Ballads*	
1867	Ibsen, *Peer Gynt*	Second Reform Bill
1868		Gladstone becomes Prime Minister
1869	Mill, *The Subjection of Women*	
1870	Death of Dickens	Franco-Prussian War Education Act brings education for all
1871	Darwin, *The Descent of Man*	Trade unions legalized
1874		Disraeli becomes Prime Minister The modern bicycle arrives
1876	James's novels begin to be published	
1878		Edison invents the incandescent electric lamp

Year	Age	Life
1879	39	His short story, 'The Distracted Preacher', is published
1880	40	*The Trumpet-Major*. Is taken ill for several months
1881	41	*A Laodicean*
1882	42	*Two on a Tower*. Visits Paris
1885	45	Moves into Max Gate, house on outskirts of Dorchester. Lives there for the rest of his life
1886	46	*The Mayor of Casterbridge*. Sees Impressionist paintings in London
1887	47	*The Woodlanders*. Visits France and Italy
1888	48	*Wessex Tales*, his first collection of short stories, and an essay on 'The Profitable Reading of Fiction'
1890	50	An essay, 'Candour in English Fiction'
1891	51	*Tess of the d'Urbervilles*; *A Group of Noble Dames* (short stories); an essay, 'The Science of Fiction'
1892	52	Death of Hardy's father
1893	53	On visit to Ireland meets Florence Henniker, for whom he develops a great affection
1894	54	*Life's Little Ironies* (short stories)
1895	55	*Jude the Obscure*
1895–6		First collected edition of novels, entitled 'Wessex Novels'

Year	Literary Context	Historical Events
1879	James Murray becomes editor of what was later to become *The Oxford English Dictionary* Ibsen, *A Doll's House*	
1880	Death of George Eliot Zola, *Nana*	
1881	Revised Version of New Testament	Married Women's Property Act
1882	Deaths of Darwin, D. G. Rossetti and Trollope	Daimler's petrol engine
1885	Birth of D. H. Lawrence	Salisbury becomes Prime Minister
1886	Death of William Barnes, friend of Hardy, poet, philologist, polymath	
1887	Strindberg, *The Father*	
1888	Death of Arnold Birth of T. S. Eliot About now the works of Kipling and Yeats begin to be published	
1889	Deaths of Browning, G. M. Hopkins and Wilkie Collins	
1890	Death of Newman	First underground railway in London
1891	Shaw, *Quintessence of Ibsenism*	
1892	Death of Tennyson	Gladstone Prime Minister
1893	Pinero, *The Second Mrs Tanqueray*	Independent Labour Party set up
1894	Deaths of Stevenson and Pater	Rosebery becomes Prime Minister
1895	Conrad's first novel, *Almayer's Folly* Wilde, *The Importance of Being Earnest*	Marconi's 'wireless' telegraphy

Year	Age	Life
1896	56	Ceases novel-writing and returns to poetry
1897	57	*The Well-Beloved*, much revised after publication as a serial in 1892
1898	58	*Wessex Poems* (51 poems): Hardy's first book of verse, including his own illustrations
1901	61	*Poems of the Past and the Present* (99 poems)
1902	62	Macmillan become his main publishers
1904	64	*The Dynasts*, Part I. Death of his mother, Jemima
1905	65	Receives honorary doctorate from Aberdeen University, the first of several
1906	66	*The Dynasts*, Part II. About now meets Florence Dugdale
1908	68	*The Dynasts*, Part III. Edits a selection of Barnes's verse
1909	69	*Time's Laughingstocks* (94 poems)
1910	70	Awarded the Order of Merit
1911	71	Ceases spending 'the season' in London
1912	72	Death of his wife, Emma. The Wessex Edition of his works is published by Macmillan
1913	73	*A Changed Man and Other Tales*. Revisits Cornwall and the scenes of his courtship of Emma
1914	74	*Satires of Circumstance* (107 poems). Marries Florence Dugdale

Year	Literary Context	Historical Events
1896	Housman, *A Shropshire Lad*	
1898	Wells, *The War of the Worlds*	The Curies discover radium
1899		The Boer War begins
1900	Deaths of Ruskin and Wilde	
1901		Death of Queen Victoria, who is succeeded by Edward VII
1902	Zola dies; Hardy laments his death	Balfour becomes Prime Minister
1903		Wright brothers make first flight in aeroplane with engine
1904	Chekhov, *The Cherry Orchard*	
1906		Liberals win election
1907	Kipling is awarded Nobel Prize	
1908		Asquith becomes Prime Minister
1909	Deaths of Swinburne and Meredith	
1910		Death of Edward VII, who is succeeded by George V
1911	Bennett, *Clayhanger* Brooke, *Poems*	
1912		Sinking of *Titanic*
1913	Lawrence, *Sons and Lovers*	First Morris Oxford car
1914	Pound editor of the first anthology of imagist poetry Frost, *North of Boston*	The First World War begins

Year	Age	Life
1915	75	Death of his sister, Mary
1916	76	*Selected Poems of Thomas Hardy* edited by Hardy himself
1917	77	*Moments of Vision* (159 poems). Begins to write his autobiography with intention that Florence should publish it under her own name after his death
1919–20	79	A de luxe edition of his work, the Mellstock Edition, is published
1920 onwards	80	Max Gate becomes a place of pilgrimage for hundreds of admirers
1922	82	*Late Lyrics and Earlier* (151 poems)
1923	83	*The Queen of Cornwall* (a poetic play)
1924	84	Hardy's adaptation of *Tess* performed in Dorchester
1925	85	*Human Shows* (152 poems)
1928	88	Hardy dies on 11 January, part buried in Westminster Abbey, part at the family church at Stinsford. *Winter Words* (105 poems) is published posthumously. *The Early Life of Thomas Hardy*, his disguised autobiography, is published
1930		*The Later Years of Thomas Hardy*, the second volume of the autobiography, is published. *Collected Poems* (918 poems) followed by *Complete Poems* (947 poems) in 1976
1937		Death of Hardy's second wife, Florence

Year	Literary Context	Historical Events
1915	Virginia Woolf, *The Voyage Out*	
1916	Death of James Lawrence's *The Rainbow* seized by the police	Lloyd George becomes Prime Minister
1917		The Russian Revolution
1918	Sassoon, *Counter-Attack* Hopkins, *Poems*	The First World War ends Women over thirty given the vote
1919		Treaty of Versailles First woman MP
1920	Edward Thomas, *Collected Poems* Owen, *Poems*	First meeting of the League of Nations
1922	Eliot, *The Waste Land* Joyce, *Ulysses*	Mussolini comes to power in Italy Women are given equality in divorce proceedings
1924	Forster, *A Passage to India*	Ramsay MacDonald forms first Labour Government Stalin becomes Soviet Dictator
1926	T. E. Lawrence, *Seven Pillars of Wisdom*	The General Strike
1927		Lindbergh makes first crossing of the Atlantic by air
1928	Lawrence's *Lady Chatterley's Lover* privately printed in Florence	

Introduction

Until quite recently, most people probably thought of Hardy as a novelist, though they were probably also aware that he had written a number of poems, some of which had become familiar anthology-pieces. The truth is that he was in his own eyes first and foremost a poet: it was as a poet that he began to write in his teens and, in his twenties, to offer his work (entirely without success) to editors, and although he devoted himself to fiction for a quarter of a century he returned to poetry as soon as circumstances permitted and wrote little else during the last thirty years of his long life. In his later years poetry, always a vocation for Hardy, became a profession, and he would go to his study each morning after breakfast to write poems as other elderly gentlemen might settle down to the newspaper and the crossword. Like Tennyson and Yeats, he wrote many of his finest poems in his old age, and his last verses were, quite literally, dictated on his deathbed.

The result is that his career as a poet, though not without interruptions, was exceptionally long: his surviving poems cover some seventy years. He was also remarkably prolific, his *Collected Poems* running to nearly 950 items. The present selection contains more than one hundred poems taken from all of the eight volumes of Hardy's verse originally published between 1898 and 1928. It includes many of the best known but also some that readers may find pleasure in encountering for the first time.

Recognition of Hardy's status – surely unique among English authors – as a major novelist who was also a major poet did not come quickly, and if one reads some of the poems he wrote in his twenties it is not difficult to see why the magazine editors to whom they were submitted unanimously rejected them. For he was, in the mid-Victorian age, a modern poet born out of his time. Some of his earliest surviving poems were written at about the time Tennyson published his hugely successful *Enoch Arden* (1864), and the contrast between the work of the Laureate and that of the unknown young poet from Dorset is very striking. Hardy rejected Tennysonian smoothness and musicality in favour of a style that is often wilfully harsh and disconcertingly experimental. Instead of conforming to traditional post-Romantic notions concerning the language of poetry, he flings open the door to admit into his poems almost any and every kind of word, obscure, archaic, technical, dialect, colloquial – and even invented. (The first poem in this selection contains the word 'unblooms', coined for the purpose but characteristic of one dominant Hardyan mood in its bleak negativity.) This habit of startling the reader by a totally unexpected choice of word persisted: in 'Nobody Comes', written nearly sixty years later, a car 'whangs along'.

So there is, with remarkable consistency throughout Hardy's work as a poet, a resistance to the smoothly and soothingly musical as well as to the regular and the predictable. At the same time he was often moved by a genuine lyric impulse. 'Any little old song/ Will do for me' he writes in one of the briefest but most touching of the poems in this selection, and music always meant a great deal to him. His family had a strong tradition of music-making and he learned very early to play the violin (as 'The Self-Unseeing' movingly recalls) as well as absorbing a wide range of available musical experience from folksong and dances to hymns and metrical psalms. His later musical tastes ranged from fashionable waltzes and quadrilles to the operas of Verdi. Many of his poems reflect, in subject-matter and sometimes also in form, different facets of his love of music.

As the dialogue in his novels often shows, he also had a keen ear for natural speech, and for Hardy a poem often grew from a scrap of spontaneous utterance that, apparently banal in itself, nevertheless possessed its own inherent music. 'It never looks like summer here' is a remark that any of us might unthinkingly make, but it becomes the starting-point for one of his most haunting poems. Again, 'Thoughts of Phena' begins as a natural rumination, like a man talking to himself, and many other poems convey this impression of being not so much acts of communication as a kind of thinking aloud.

Hardy not only wrote many poems, he wrote many kinds of poetry: love poems, ballad poems, animal poems, war (or anti-war) poems, comic and satirical poems, poems about places, poems about the seasons and the weather, poems about rural life and work, poems about his family and friends and about other poets. Some of his poems bring together his two careers, as poet and novelist, by using material that also appears in his fiction: 'We Field-Women' will strike a chord for anyone who has read *Tess of the d'Urbervilles*, while both 'Childhood among the Ferns' and 'Midnight on the Great Western' versify, with modifications, memorable passages in *Jude the Obscure*.

Of all these categories perhaps the most important is love poetry, and here we need to recall that much of Hardy's poetry is the work of an old man. Already in his fifties Hardy was lamenting the ravages of time: see, for an exceptionally fine example somewhat unexpectedly using a metrical form from *Hymns Ancient and Modern*, 'I Look Into My Glass', which originally stood prominently on the last page of his very first collection of poems. Of course he was not to know that he would live for another thirty years, or that these would be years of extraordinary creativity. In his last novels, especially *Tess of the d'Urbervilles* and *Jude the Obscure*, he had shown a preoccupation with families that seemed to have exhausted their vitality, and his own childlessness may have been a grief to him. But if his real family was the books he produced, he remained fertile to the very end.

In his poetry, however, love is most often a matter either of vanished joys or of missed opportunities. His finest outpouring, in his early seventies, was the sequence to which he gave the unrevealing title *Poems of 1912–13*. His wife Emma had often been a source of exasperation and embarrassment in the later years of their marriage, and they had drifted irrevocably apart; but her death on 27 November 1912 released memories of the distant past – and especially of their romantic first meeting and courtship in Cornwall – and the poems flowed with them. In a curious act of atonement and self-punishment that must also have served to invigorate his poetic inspiration, he travelled to Cornwall in early March 1913 to revisit the scenes of vanished joy. Always possessing a strong feeling for an anniversary, he set out on 6 March 1913, which was, as he noted, 'almost to a day' forty-three years after the first journey to Cornwall, magically relived in 'When I Set Out for Lyonnesse'. The experience was, as he admitted, 'very painful', but its poetic harvest was significant – and revisiting was, for Hardy, always to be a peculiarly fruitful activity.

In a sense, though, the subject of the poems addressed to Emma Hardy after her death is not so much love as loss: the dead woman has far more power to move and inspire him than the living one had. They are very private poems, and it remains a cause for astonishment that Hardy, a man of intense reserve, should have printed them; on the other hand, though Emma is quite clearly the subject, her name is nowhere mentioned. Repeatedly, in reading a Hardy poem, we have a sense of intrusion – of gaining access, almost illicitly and improperly, to secret feelings. Certainly the *Poems of 1912–13* seem to be less addressed to a reader than words spoken to himself, or to his wife's ghost.

Throughout his life, Hardy had the knack of conceiving romantic feelings towards women who failed to reciprocate his attachment. Sometimes, indeed – what might be called, using a phrase from his autobiography, the girl-in-the-omnibus complex – they were unaware of his very existence. 'To Lizbie Browne' and 'To Louisa in the Lane' show that the habit was formed very early: even as a boy Hardy became something of a specialist in unrequited love. In the 1890s, his romantic attachment to Florence Henniker, a married woman of the upper classes, is poignantly reflected in 'A Broken Appointment' and other poems. The love affairs that never went beyond fantasizing on Hardy's part were potent in stimulating the creative flow. And as with Emma, death could also be a powerful stimulus. Hardy may or may not have had a love affair with his cousin Tryphena Sparks: what is quite certain is that it was necessary for her to die before he was ready to write his tender and delicately rhythmical 'Thoughts of Phena'. A different kind of love, the deep attachment to members of his family, is evident in several poems in this selection that refer to Hardy's mother, sister and grandmother and to his parents' courtship. Again, it is striking that these poems, like others referring to friends ('The Five Students', 'The Last Signal') almost invariably refer to the dead rather than the living. It is as if, for Hardy, we can see our loved ones steadily and whole, and properly understand our feelings towards them, only after their death.

Of other subjects for poetry, nature, the countryside, and those who live and work therein are frequent, as one might expect from the author of the 'Wessex Novels'. Birds, for instance, are a favourite theme. But the ostensible subject of a Hardy poem is often no more than a point of departure for its real theme: 'The Darkling Thrush', say, is not just a poem about a bird but a profound and wide-ranging meditation on time, history and faith. Another bird-poem that quickly moves from the specific to the general is 'Proud

Songsters', beautifully set by Benjamin Britten in his song-cycle *Winter Words*, which borrows the title of Hardy's final collection of verse and makes use of several other poems in this selection. This quality of relating the particular to the universal, often through strong and sharply observed visual images, is what W. H. Auden had in mind when – using an appropriately avian metaphor – he referred to Hardy's 'hawk's vision'. At the same time he is a master of the close-up, writing (in 'Afterwards' and elsewhere) of the natural scene with informed sensitivity.

Somewhat similarly, the twelve short lines of 'In Time of "The Breaking of Nations" ' offer three snapshots of rural life that, by some invisible chemistry in the spaces between them, constitute a deeply felt comment on war, history, work and love. Possibly no other short poem ever written was quite so long in the making, for we have Hardy's word for it that the idea came to him around 1870, at the time of the Franco-Prussian War, only to be embodied in verse nearly half a century later, during the Great War. Both the Boer War and the First World War generated a considerable number of poems, and in some of them Hardy seems to anticipate Wilfred Owen and other war poets in his condemnation of war's tragic futility. 'Drummer Hodge', for example, a kind of poetic equivalent of the grave of the Unknown Warrior, shows how quiet lives are disrupted and destroyed by war.

To categorize the varieties of Hardy's verse is an almost endless task, and nothing has been said of his narrative poetry. 'A Trampwoman's Tragedy', which he seems to have considered his 'most successful' poem, is a masterly example of the modern ballad. He is, too, an effective comic and satirical poet: the wry monologue 'The Curate's Kindness' and the early dialogue poem 'The Ruined Maid' are witty at the expense of conventional ideas. There are other poems that derive from his intellectual interests and his wide reading: his enthusiasm for astronomy, which provided the material for one of his novels, prompted 'At a Lunar Eclipse' and 'The Comet at Yell'ham'. Elsewhere, turning from the boundless universe to the trivial events of the individual life, he can write of simple happenings – or even, in 'Nobody Comes' and 'Faintheart on a Railway Train' – non-happenings.

For part of Hardy's profound originality as as poet is that, just as almost any and every word is a potential candidate for admission into his poetic vocabulary, he has no prejudices or inhibitions about what constitutes a proper poetic subject. This indifference to tradition and fashion made him, at a date when most of the great modernist poets were not yet born, a quiet revolutionary. He lived long enough to see the modernist age and to count a number of younger writers among his friends, but the remarkable thing is that his distinctive, off-beat and intensely personal style was established during the reign of Queen Victoria.

NORMAN PAGE

Thomas Hardy

Hap

If but some vengeful god would call to me
From up the sky, and laugh: 'Thou suffering thing,
Know that thy sorrow is my ecstasy,
That thy love's loss is my hate's profiting!'

Then would I bear it, clench myself, and die,
Steeled by the sense of ire unmerited;
Half-eased in that a Powerfuller than I
Had willed and meted me the tears I shed.

But not so. How arrives it joy lies slain,
And why unblooms the best hope ever sown?
– Crass Casualty obstructs the sun and rain,
And dicing Time for gladness casts a moan. . . .
These purblind Doomsters had as readily strown
Blisses about my pilgrimage as pain.

1866

Neutral Tones

We stood by a pond that winter day,
And the sun was white, as though chidden of God,
And a few leaves lay on the starving sod;
    – They had fallen from an ash, and were gray.

Your eyes on me were as eyes that rove
Over tedious riddles of years ago;
And some words played between us to and fro
    On which lost the more by our love.

The smile on your mouth was the deadest thing
Alive enough to have strength to die;

And a grin of bitterness swept thereby
  Like an ominous bird a-wing. . . .

Since then, keen lessons that love deceives,
And wrings with wrong, have shaped to me
Your face, and the God-curst sun, and a tree,
  And a pond edged with grayish leaves.

1867

Friends Beyond

William Dewy, Tranter Reuben, Farmer Ledlow late at plough,
    Robert's kin, and John's, and Ned's,
And the Squire, and Lady Susan, lie in Mellstock churchyard
    now!

'Gone,' I call them, gone for good, that group of local hearts and
    heads;
    Yet at mothy curfew-tide,
And at midnight when the noon-heat breathes it back from walls
    and leads,

They've a way of whispering to me – fellow-wight who yet
    abide –
    In the mited, measured note
Of a ripple under archways, or a lone cave's stillicide:

'We have triumphed: this achievement turns the bane to
    antidote,
    Unsuccesses to success,
Many thought-worn eves and morrows to a morrow free of
    thought.

'No more need we corn and clothing, feel of old terrestrial stress;
      Chill detraction stirs no sigh;
Fear of death has even bygone us: death gave all that we possess.'

W.D. – 'Ye mid burn the old bass-viol that I set such value by.'
Squire. – 'You may hold the manse in fee,
      You may wed my spouse, may let my children's memory of
         me die.'

Lady S. – 'You may have my rich brocades, my laces; take each
         household key;
      Ransack coffer, desk, bureau;
   Quiz the few poor treasures hid there, con the letters kept by
      me.'

Far. – 'Ye mid zell my favourite heifer, ye mid let the charlock
      grow,
      Foul the grinterns, give up thrift.'
Far. Wife. – 'If ye break my best blue china, children, I shan't
      care or ho.'

All. – 'We've no wish to hear the tidings, how the people's
         fortunes shift;
      What your daily doings are;
   Who are wedded, born, divided; if your lives beat slow or
      swift.

'Curious not the least are we if our intents your make or mar,
      If you quire to our old tune,
If the City stage still passes, if the weirs still roar afar.'

– Thus, with very gods' composure, freed those crosses late and
         soon
      Which, in life, the Trine allow
(Why, none witteth), and ignoring all that haps beneath the
      moon,

William Dewy, Tranter Reuben, Farmer Ledlow late at plough,
      Robert's kin, and John's, and Ned's,
And the Squire, and Lady Susan, murmur mildly to me now.

Thoughts of Phena*

At News of Her Death

Not a line of her writing have I,
　　Not a thread of her hair,
No mark of her late time as dame in her dwelling, whereby
　　I may picture her there;
　　And in vain do I urge my unsight
　　　To conceive my lost prize
At her close, whom I knew when her dreams were upbrimming
　　　with light,
　　And with laughter her eyes.

What scenes spread around her last days,
　　Sad, shining, or dim?
Did her gifts and compassions enray and enarch her sweet ways
　　With an aureate nimb?
　　Or did life-light decline from her years,
　　　And mischances control
Her full day-star; unease, or regret, or forebodings, or fears
　　Disennoble her soul?

Thus I do but the phantom retain
　　Of the maiden of yore
As my relic; yet haply the best of her – fined in my brain
　　It may be the more
　　That no line of her writing have I,
　　　Nor a thread of her hair,
No mark of her late time as dame in her dwelling, whereby
　　I may picture her there.

March 1890

Nature's Questioning

When I look forth at dawning, pool,
    Field, flock, and lonely tree,
    All seem to gaze at me
Like chastened children sitting silent in a school;

Their faces dulled, constrained, and worn,
    As though the master's ways
    Through the long teaching days
Had cowed them till their early zest was overborne.

Upon them stirs in lippings mere
    (As if once clear in call,
    But now scarce breathed at all) –
'We wonder, ever wonder, why we find us here!

'Has some Vast Imbecility,
    Mighty to build and blend,
    But impotent to tend,
Framed us in jest, and left us now to hazardry?

'Or come we of an Automaton
    Unconscious of our pains? . . .
    Or are we live remains
Of Godhead dying downwards, brain and eye now gone?

'Or is it that some high Plan betides,
    As yet not understood,
    Of Evil stormed by Good,
We the Forlorn Hope over which Achievement strides?'

Thus things around. No answerer I. . . .
    Meanwhile the winds, and rains,
    And Earth's old glooms and pains
Are still the same, and Life and Death are neighbours nigh.

In a Eweleaze near Weatherbury*

The years have gathered grayly
    Since I danced upon this leaze
With one who kindled gaily
    Love's fitful ecstasies!
But despite the term as teacher,
    I remain what I was then
In each essential feature
    Of the fantasies of men.

Yet I note the little chisel
    Of never-napping Time
Defacing wan and grizzel
    The blazon of my prime.
When at night he thinks me sleeping
    I feel him boring sly
Within my bones, and heaping
    Quaintest pains for by-and-by.

Still, I'd go the world with Beauty,
    I would laugh with her and sing,
I would shun divinest duty
    To resume her worshipping.
But she'd scorn my brave endeavour,
    She would not balm the breeze
By murmuring 'Thine for ever!'
    As she did upon this leaze.

1890

I Look Into My Glass

I look into my glass,
And view my wasting skin,
And say, 'Would God it came to pass
My heart had shrunk as thin!'

For then, I, undistrest
By hearts grown cold to me,
Could lonely wait my endless rest
With equanimity.

But Time, to make me grieve,
Part steals, lets part abide;
And shakes this fragile frame at eve
With throbbings of noontide.

At the War Office, London

(Affixing the Lists of Killed and Wounded: December 1899)

I

Last year I called this world of gaingivings
The darkest thinkable, and questioned sadly
If my own land could heave its pulse less gladly
So charged it seemed with circumstance that brings
The tragedy of things.

II

Yet at that censured time no heart was rent
Or feature blanched of parent, wife or daughter
By hourly posted sheets of scheduled slaughter;
Death waited Nature's wont; Peace smiled unshent
From Ind to Occident.

A Christmas Ghost-Story

South of the Line, inland from far Durban,
A mouldering soldier lies – your countryman.
Awry and doubled up are his gray bones,
And on the breeze his puzzled phantom moans
Nightly to clear Canopus: 'I would know
By whom and when the All-Earth-gladdening Law
Of Peace, brought in by that Man Crucified,
Was ruled to be inept, and set aside?
And what of logic or of truth appears
In tacking 'Anno Domini' to the years?
Near twenty-hundred liveried thus have hied,
But tarries yet the Cause for which He died.'

Christmas Eve 1899

Drummer Hodge*

I

They throw in Drummer Hodge, to rest
    Uncoffined – just as found:
His landmark is a kopje-crest
    That breaks the veldt around;
And foreign constellations west
    Each night above his mound.

II

Young Hodge the Drummer never knew –
    Fresh from his Wessex home –
The meaning of the broad Karoo,
    The Bush, the dusty loam,
And why uprose to nightly view
    Strange stars amid the gloom.

III
Yet portion of that unknown plain
    Will Hodge for ever be;
His homely Northern breast and brain
    Grow to some Southern tree,
And strange-eyed constellations reign
    His stars eternally.

Shelley's Skylark*

(The neighbourhood of Leghorn: March 1887)

Somewhere afield here something lies
In Earth's oblivious eyeless trust
That moved a poet to prophecies –
A pinch of unseen, unguarded dust:

The dust of the lark that Shelley heard,
And made immortal through times to be; –
Though it only lived like another bird,
And knew not its immortality:

Lived its meek life; then, one day, fell –
A little ball of feather and bone;
And how it perished, when piped farewell,
And where it wastes, are alike unknown.

Maybe it rests in the loam I view,
Maybe it throbs in a myrtle's green,
Maybe it sleeps in the coming hue
Of a grape on the slopes of yon inland scene.

Go find it, faeries, go and find
That tiny pinch of priceless dust,
And bring a casket silver-lined,
And framed of gold that gems encrust;

And we will lay it safe therein,
And consecrate it to endless time;
For it inspired a bard to win
Ecstatic heights in thought and rhyme.

On an Invitation to the United States

I

My ardours for emprize nigh lost
Since Life has bared its bones to me,
I shrink to seek a modern coast
Whose riper times have yet to be;
Where the new regions claim them free
From that long drip of human tears
Which peoples old in tragedy
Have left upon the centuried years.

II

For, wonning in these ancient lands,
Enchased and lettered as a tomb,
And scored with prints of perished hands,
And chronicled with dates of doom,
Though my own Being bear no bloom
I trace the lives such scenes enshrine,
Give past exemplars present room,
And their experience count as mine.

At a Lunar Eclipse

Thy shadow, Earth, from Pole to Central Sea,
Now steals along upon the Moon's meek shine
In even monochrome and curving line
Of imperturbable serenity.

How shall I link such sun-cast symmetry
With the torn troubled form I know as thine,
That profile, placid as a brow divine,
With continents of moil and misery?

And can immense Mortality but throw
So small a shade, and Heaven's high human scheme
Be hemmed within the coasts yon arc implies?

Is such the stellar gauge of earthly show,
Nation at war with nation, brains that teem,
Heroes, and women fairer than the skies?

To Lizbie Browne*

I

Dear Lizbie Browne,
Where are you now?
In sun, in rain? –
Or is your brow
Past joy, past pain,
Dear Lizbie Browne?

II

Sweet Lizbie Browne,
How you could smile,
How you could sing! –
How archly wile

In glance-giving,
Sweet Lizbie Browne!

III

And, Lizbie Browne,
Who else had hair
Bay-red as yours,
Or flesh so fair
Bred out of doors,
Sweet Lizbie Browne?

IV

When, Lizbie Browne,
You had just begun
To be endeared
By stealth to one,
You disappeared
My Lizbie Browne!

V

Ay, Lizbie Browne,
So swift your life,
And mine so slow,
You were a wife
Ere I could show
Love, Lizbie Browne.

VI

Still, Lizbie Browne,
You won, they said,
The best of men
When you were wed. . . .
Where went you then,
O Lizbie Browne?

VII

Dear Lizbie Browne,
I should have thought,
'Girls ripen fast,'
And coaxed and caught

You ere you passed,
Dear Lizbie Browne!

VIII

But, Lizbie Browne,
I let you slip;
Shaped not a sign;
Touched never your lip
With lip of mine,
Lost Lizbie Browne!

IX

So, Lizbie Browne,
When on a day
Men speak of me
As not, you'll say,
'And who was he?' –
Yes, Lizbie Browne!

A Broken Appointment*

You did not come,
And marching Time drew on, and wore me numb. –
Yet less for loss of your dear presence there
Than that I thus found lacking in your make
That high compassion which can overbear
Reluctance for pure lovingkindness' sake
Grieved I, when, as the hope-hour stroked its sum,
You did not come.

You love not me,
And love alone can lend you loyalty;
– I know and knew it. But, unto the store
Of human deeds divine in all but name,
Was it not worth a little hour or more
To add yet this. Once you, a woman, came
To soothe a time-torn man; even though it be
You love not me?

I Need Not Go

I need not go
Through sleet and snow
To where I know
She waits for me;
She will tarry me there
Till I find it fair,
And have time to spare
From company.

When I've overgot
The world somewhat,
When things cost not
Such stress and strain,
Is soon enough
By cypress sough
To tell my Love
I am come again.

And if some day,
When none cries nay,
I still delay
To seek her side,
(Though ample measure
Of fitting leisure
Await my pleasure)
She will not chide.

What – not upbraid me
That I delayed me,
Nor ask what stayed me
So long? Ah, no! –
New cares may claim me,
New loves inflame me,
She will not blame me,
But suffer it so.

Birds at Winter Nightfall

(Triolet)

Around the house the flakes fly faster,
And all the berries now are gone
From holly and cotonea-aster
Around the house. The flakes fly – faster
Shutting indoors that crumb-outcaster
We used to see upon the lawn
Around the house. The flakes fly faster,
And all the berries now are gone!

Max Gate

The Puzzled Game-Birds

(Triolet)

They are not those who used to feed us
When we were young – they cannot be –
These shapes that now bereave and bleed us?
They are not those who used to feed us,
For did we then cry, they would heed us.
– If hearts can house such treachery
They are not those who used to feed us
When we were young – they cannot be!

The Last Chrysanthemum

Why should this flower delay so long
    To show its tremulous plumes?
Now is the time of plaintive robin-song,
    When flowers are in their tombs.

Through the slow summer, when the sun
    Called to each frond and whorl
That all he could for flowers was being done,
    Why did it not uncurl?

It must have felt that fervid call
    Although it took no heed,
Waking but now, when leaves like corpses fall,
    And saps all retrocede.

Too late its beauty, lonely thing,
    The season's shine is spent,
Nothing remains for it but shivering
    In tempests turbulent.

Had it a reason for delay,
    Dreaming in witlessness
That for a bloom so delicately gay
    Winter would stay its stress?

– I talk as if the thing were born
With sense to work its mind;
Yet it is but one mask of many worn
By the Great Face behind.

The Darkling Thrush*

I leant upon a coppice gate
    When Frost was spectre-gray,
And Winter's dregs made desolate
    The weakening eye of day.
The tangled bine-stems scored the sky
    Like strings of broken lyres,
And all mankind that haunted nigh
    Had sought their household fires.

The land's sharp features seemed to be
    The Century's corpse outleant,
His crypt the cloudy canopy,
    The wind his death-lament.
The ancient pulse of germ and birth
    Was shrunken hard and dry,
And every spirit upon earth
    Seemed fervourless as I.

At once a voice arose among
    The bleak twigs overhead
In a full-hearted evensong
    Of joy illimited;
An aged thrush, frail, gaunt, and small,
    In blast-beruffled plume,
Had chosen thus to fling his soul
    Upon the growing gloom.

So little cause for carolings
    Of such ecstatic sound
Was written on terrestrial things
    Afar or nigh around,
That I could think there trembled through
    His happy good-night air
Some blessed Hope, whereof he knew
    And I was unaware.

31 December 1900

The Comet at Yell'ham*

I

It heads far over Yell'ham Plain,
   And we, from Yell'ham Height,
Stand and regard its fiery train,
   So soon to swim from sight.

II

It will return long years hence, when
   As now its strange swift shine
Will fall on Yell'ham, but not then
   On that sweet form of thine.

The Levelled Churchyard

'O Passenger, pray list and catch
   Our sighs and piteous groans,
Half stifled in this jumbled patch
   Of wrenched memorial stones!

'We late-lamented, resting here,
   Are mixed to human jam,
And each to each exclaims in fear,
   "I know not which I am!"

'The wicked people have annexed
   The verses on the good;
A roaring drunkard sports the text
   Teetotal Tommy should!

'Where we are huddled none can trace,
   And if our names remain,
They pave some path or porch or place
   Where we have never lain!

'Here's not a modest maiden elf
    But dreads the final Trumpet,
Lest half of her should rise herself,
    And half some sturdy strumpet!

'From restorations of Thy fane,
    From smoothings of Thy sward,
From zealous Churchmen's pick and plane
    Deliver us O Lord! Amen!'

1882

The Ruined Maid

'O 'Melia, my dear, this does everything crown!
Who could have supposed I should meet you in Town?
And whence such fair garments, such prosperi-ty?' –
'O didn't you know I'd been ruined?' said she.

– 'You left us in tatters, without shoes or socks,
Tired of digging potatoes, and spudding up docks;
And now you've gay bracelets and bright feathers three!' –
'Yes: that's how we dress when we're ruined,' said she.

– 'At home in the barton you said "thee" and "thou",
And "thik oon", and "theäs oon", and "t'other"; but now
Your talking quite fits 'ee for high compa-ny!' –
'Some polish is gained with one's ruin,' said she.

– 'Your hands were like paws then, your face blue and bleak
But now I'm bewitched by your delicate cheek,
And your little gloves fit as on any la-dy!' –
'We never do work when we're ruined,' said she.

– 'You used to call home-life a hag-ridden dream,
And you'd sigh, and you'd sock; but at present you seem

To know not of megrims or melancho-ly!' –
'True. One's pretty lively when ruined,' said she.

– 'I wish I had feathers, a fine sweeping gown,
And a delicate face, and could strut about Town!' –
'My dear – a raw country girl, such as you be,
Cannot quite expect that. You ain't ruined,' said she.

Westbourne Park Villas, 1866

The Self-Unseeing

Here is the ancient floor,
Footworn and hollowed and thin,
Here was the former door
Where the dead feet walked in.

She sat here in her chair,
Smiling into the fire;
He who played stood there,
Bowing it higher and higher.

Childlike, I danced in a dream;
Blessings emblazoned that day;
Everything glowed with a gleam;
Yet we were looking away!

A Trampwoman's Tragedy*

(182–)

I

From Wynyard's Gap the livelong day,
    The livelong day,
We beat afoot the northward way
    We had travelled times before.
The sun-blaze burning on our backs,
Our shoulders sticking to our packs,
By fosseway, fields, and turnpike tracks
    We skirted sad Sedge-Moor.

II

Full twenty miles we jaunted on,
    We jaunted on, –
My fancy-man, and jeering John,
    And Mother Lee, and I.
And, as the sun drew down to west,
We climbed the toilsome Poldon crest,
And saw, of landskip sights the best,
    The inn that beamed thereby.

III

For months we had padded side by side,
    Ay, side by side
Through the Great Forest, Blackmoor wide,
    And where the Parret ran.
We'd faced the gusts on Mendip ridge,
Had crossed the Yeo unhelped by bridge,
Been stung by every Marshwood midge,
    I and my fancy-man.

IV

Lone inns we loved, my man and I,
    My man and I;
'King Stag', 'Windwhistle' high and dry,
    'The Horse' on Hintock Green,

The cosy house at Wynyard's Gap,
'The Hut' renowned on Bredy Knap,
And many another wayside tap
    Where folk might sit unseen.

V

Now as we trudged – O deadly day,
    O deadly day! –
I teased my fancy-man in play
    And wanton idleness.
I walked alongside jeering John,
I laid his hand my waist upon;
I would not bend my glances on
    My lover's dark distress.

VI

Thus Poldon top at last we won,
    At last we won,
And gained the inn at sink of sun
    Far-famed as 'Marshal's Elm'.
Beneath us figured tor and lea,
From Mendip to the western sea –
I doubt if finer sight there be
    Within this royal realm.

VII

Inside the settle all a-row –
    All four a row
We sat, I next to John, to show
    That he had wooed and won.
And then he took me on his knee,
And swore it was his turn to be
My favoured mate, and Mother Lee
    Passed to my former one.

VIII

Then in a voice I had never heard,
    I had never heard,
My only Love to me: 'One word,
    My lady, if you please!

Whose is the child you are like to bear? –
His? After all my months o' care?'
God knows 'twas not! But, O despair!
    I nodded – still to tease.

IX

Then up he sprung, and with his knife –
    And with his knife
He let out jeering Johnny's life,
    Yes; there, at set of sun.
The slant ray through the window nigh
Gilded John's blood and glazing eye,
Ere scarcely Mother Lee and I
    Knew that the deed was done.

X

The taverns tell the gloomy tale,
    The gloomy tale,
How that at Ivel-chester jail
    My love, my sweetheart swung;
Though stained till now by no misdeed
Save one horse ta'en in time o' need;
(Blue Jimmy stole right many a steed
    Ere his last fling he flung.)

XI

Thereaft I walked the world alone,
    Alone, alone!
On his death-day I gave my groan
    And dropt his dead-born child.
'Twas nigh the jail, beneath a tree,
None tending me; for Mother Lee
Had died at Glaston, leaving me
    Unfriended on the wild.

XII

And in the night as I lay weak,
    As I lay weak,
The leaves a-falling on my cheek,
    The red moon low declined –

The ghost of him I'd die to kiss
Rose up and said: 'Ah, tell me this!
Was the child mine, or was it his?
    Speak, that I rest may find!'

XIII

O doubt not but I told him then,
    I told him then,
That I had kept me from all men
    Since we joined lips and swore.
Whereat he smiled, and thinned away
As the wind stirred to call up day . . .
– 'Tis past! And here alone I stray
    Haunting the Western Moor.

April 1902

A Sunday Morning Tragedy*

(circa 186–)

I bore a daughter flower-fair,
In Pydel Vale, alas for me;
I joyed to mother one so rare,
But dead and gone I now would be.

Men looked and loved her as she grew,
And she was won, alas for me;
She told me nothing, but I knew,
And saw that sorrow was to be.

I knew that one had made her thrall,
A thrall to him, alas for me;
And then, at last, she told me all,
And wondered what her end would be.

She owned that she had loved too well,
Had loved too well, unhappy she,

And bore a secret time would tell,
Though in her shroud she'd sooner be.

I plodded to her sweetheart's door
In Pydel Vale, alas for me.
I pleaded with him, pleaded sore,
To save her from her misery.

He frowned, and swore he could not wed,
Seven times he swore it could not be;
'Poverty's worse than shame,' he said,
Till all my hope went out of me.

'I've packed my traps to sail the main' –
Roughly he spake, alas did he –
'Wessex beholds me not again,
'Tis worse than any jail would be!'

– There was a shepherd whom I knew,
A subtle man, alas for me:
I sought him all the pastures through,
Though better I had ceased to be.

. I traced him by his lantern light,
And gave him hint, alas for me,
Of how she found her in the plight
That is so scorned in Christendie,

'Is there an herb . . . ?' I asked. 'Or none?'
Yes, thus I asked him desperately.
'– There is,' he said; 'A certain one. . . .'
Would he had sworn that none knew he!

'To-morrow I will walk your way,'
He hinted low, alas for me. –
Fieldwards I gazed throughout next day;
Now fields I never more would see!

The sunset-shine, as curfew strook,
As curfew strook beyond the lea,

Lit his white smock and gleaming crook,
While slowly he drew near to me.

He pulled from underneath his smock
The herb I sought, my curse to be —
'At times I use it in my flock,'
He said, and hope waxed strong in me.

''Tis meant.to balk ill-motherings' —
(Ill-motherings! Why should they be?) —
'If not, would God have sent such things?'
So spoke the shepherd unto me.

That night I watched the poppling brew,
With bended back and hand on knee:
I stirred it till the dawnlight grew,
And the wind whiffled wailfully.

'This scandal shall be slain,' said I,
'That lours upon her innocency:
I'll give all whispering tongues the lie;' —
But worse than whispers was to be.

'Here's physic for untimely fruit,'
I said to her, alas for me,
Early that morn in fond salute;
And in my grave I now would be.

— Next Sunday came, with sweet church chimes
In Pydel Vale, alas for me:
I went into her room betimes;
No more may such a Sunday be!

'Mother, instead of rescue nigh,'
She faintly breathed, alas for me,
'I feel as I were like to die,
And underground soon, soon should be.'

From church that noon the people walked
In twos and threes, alas for me,

Showed their new raiment – smiled and talked,
Though sackcloth-clad I longed to be.

Came to my door her lover's friends,
And cheerful cried, alas for me,
'Right glad are we he makes amends,
For never a sweeter bride can be.'

My mouth dried, as 'twere scorched within,
Dried at their words, alas for me:
More and more neighbours crowded in,
(O why should mothers ever be!)

'Ha-ha! Such well-kept news!' laughed they,
Yes – so they laughed, alas for me.
'Whose banns were called in church to-day?' –
Christ, how I wished my soul could flee!

'Where is she? O the stealthy miss,'
Still bantered they, alas for me,
'To keep a wedding close as this. . . .'
Ay, Fortune worked thus wantonly!

'But you are pale – you did not know?'
They archly asked, alas for me,
I stammered, 'Yes – some days – ago,'
While coffined clay I wished to be.

''Twas done to please her, we surmise?'
(They spoke quite lightly in their glee)
'Done by him as a fond surprise?'
I thought their words would madden me.

Her lover entered. 'Where's my bird? –
My bird – my flower – my picotee?
First time of asking, soon the third!'
Ah, in my grave I well may be.

To me he whispered: 'Since your call –'
So spoke he then, alas for me –

'I've felt for her, and righted all.'
– I think of it to agony.

'She's faint to-day – tired – nothing more –'
Thus did I lie, alas for me. . . .
I called her at her chamber door
As one who scarce had strength to be.

No voice replied. I went within –
O women! scourged the worst are we. . . .
I shrieked. The others hastened in
And saw the stroke there dealt on me.

There she lay – silent, breathless, dead,
Stone dead she lay – wronged, sinless she! –
Ghost-white the cheeks once rosy-red:
Death had took her. Death took not me.

I kissed her colding face and hair,
I kissed her corpse – the bride to be! –
My punishment I cannot bear,
But pray God *not* to pity me.

January 1904

The Curate's Kindness

A Workhouse Irony

I

I thought they'd be strangers aroun' me,
    But she's to be there!
Let me jump out o' waggon and go back and drown me
    At Pummery or Ten-Hatches Weir.

II

I thought: 'Well, I've come to the Union –
    The workhouse at last –
After honest hard work all the week, and Communion
    O' Zundays, these fifty years past.

III

''Tis hard; but,' I thought, 'never mind it:
    There's gain in the end:
And when I get used to the place I shall find it
    A home, and may find there a friend.

IV

'Life there will be better than t'other,
    For peace is assured.
The men in one wing and their wives in another
    Is strictly the rule of the Board.'

V

Just then one young Pa'son arriving
    Steps up out of breath
To the side o' the waggon wherein we were driving
    To Union; and calls out and saith:

VI

'Old folks, that harsh order is altered,
    Be not sick of heart!
The Guardians they poohed and they pished and they paltered
    When urged not to keep you apart.

VII

' "It is wrong," I maintained, "to divide them,
    Near forty years wed."
"Very well, sir. We promise, then, they shall abide them
    In one wing together," they said.'

VIII

Then I sank – knew 'twas quite a foredone thing
    That misery should be
To the end! . . . To get freed of her there was the one thing
    Had made the change welcome to me.

IX

To go there was ending but badly;
    'Twas shame and 'twas pain;
'But anyhow,' thought I, 'thereby I shall gladly
    Get free of this forty years' chain.'

X

I thought they'd be strangers aroun' me;
    But she's to be there!
Let me jump out o' waggon and go back and drown me
    At Pummery or Ten-Hatches Weir.

Shut Out That Moon

Close up the casement, draw the blind,
    Shut out that stealing moon,
She wears too much the guise she wore
    Before our lutes were strewn
With years-deep dust, and names we read
    On a white stone were hewn.

Step not forth on the dew-dashed lawn
    To view the Lady's Chair,
Immense Orion's glittering form,
    The Less and Greater Bear:
Stay in; to such sights we were drawn
    When faded ones were fair.

Brush not the bough for midnight scents
    That come forth lingeringly,
And wake the same sweet sentiments
    They breathed to you and me
When living seemed a laugh, and love
    All it was said to be.

Within the common lamp-lit room
    Prison my eyes and thought;

Let dingy details crudely loom,
    Mechanic speech be wrought:
Too fragrant was Life's early bloom,
    Too tart the fruit it brought!

1967

In five-score summers! All new eyes,
New minds, new modes, new fools, new wise;
New woes to weep, new joys to prize;

With nothing left of me and you
In that live century's vivid view
Beyond a pinch of dust or two;

A century which, if not sublime,
Will show, I doubt not, at its prime,
A scope above this blinkered time.

– Yet what to me how far above?
For I would only ask thereof
That thy worm should be my worm, Love!

16 Westbourne Park Villas, 1867

The Division

Rain on the windows, creaking doors,
    With blasts that besom the green,
And I am here, and you are there,
    And a hundred miles between!

O were it but the weather, Dear,
  O were it but the miles
That summed up all our severance,
  There might be room for smiles.

But that thwart thing betwixt us twain,
  Which nothing cleaves or clears,
Is more than distance, Dear, or rain,
  And longer than the years!

1893

On the Departure Platform

We kissed at the barrier; and passing through
She left me, and moment by moment got
Smaller and smaller, until to my view
  She was but a spot;

A wee white spot of muslin fluff
That down the diminishing platform bore
Through hustling crowds of gentle and rough
  To the carriage door.

Under the lamplight's fitful glowers,
Behind dark groups from far and near,
Whose interests were apart from ours,
  She would disappear,

Then show again, till I ceased to see
That flexible form, that nebulous white;
And she who was more than my life to me
  Had vanished quite. . . .

We have penned new plans since that fair fond day,
And in season she will appear again –

Perhaps in the same soft white array –
    But never as then!

– 'And why, young man, must eternally fly
A joy you'll repeat, if you love her well?'
– O friend, nought happens twice thus; why,
    I cannot tell!

A Church Romance*

(Mellstock: circa 1835)

She turned in the high pew, until her sight
Swept the west gallery, and caught its row
Of music-men with viol, book, and bow
Against the sinking sad tower-window light.

She turned again; and in her pride's despite
One strenuous viol's inspirer seemed to throw
A message from his string to her below,
Which said: 'I claim thee as my own forthright!'

Thus their hearts' bond began, in due time signed.
And long years thence, when Age had scared Romance,
At some old attitude of his or glance
That gallery-scene would break upon her mind,
With him as minstrel, ardent, young, and trim,
Bowing 'New Sabbath' or 'Mount Ephraim'.

The Roman Road

The Roman Road runs straight and bare
As the pale parting-line in hair
Across the heath. And thoughtful men
Contrast its days of Now and Then,
And delve, and measure, and compare;
Visioning on the vacant air
Helmed legionaries, who proudly rear
The Eagle, as they pace again
      The Roman Road.

But no tall brass-helmed legionnaire
Haunts it for me. Uprises there
A mother's form upon my ken,
Guiding my infant steps, as when
We walked that ancient throughfare,
      The Roman Road.

After the Last Breath*

(J.H. 1813–1904)

There's no more to be done, or feared, or hoped;
None now need watch, speak low, and list, and tire;
No irksome crease outsmoothed, no pillow sloped
  Does she require.

Blankly we gaze. We are free to go or stay;
Our morrow's anxious plans have missed their aim;
Whether we leave to-night or wait till day
  Counts as the same.

The lettered vessels of medicaments
Seem asking wherefore we have set them here;

Each palliative its silly face presents
    As useless gear.

And yet we feel that something savours well;
We note a numb relief withheld before;
Our well-beloved is prisoner in the cell
    Of Time no more.

We see by littles now the deft achievement
Whereby she has escaped the Wrongers all,
In view of which our momentary bereavement
    Outshapes but small.

1904

One We Knew*

(M.H. 1772–1857)

She told how they used to form for the country dances –
    'The Triumph', 'The New-rigged Ship' –
To the light of the guttering wax in the panelled manses,
    And in cots to the blink of a dip.

She spoke of the wild 'poussetting' and 'allemanding'
    On carpet, on oak, and on sod;
And the two long rows of ladies and gentlemen standing,
    And the figures the couples trod.

She showed us the spot where the maypole was yearly planted,
    And where the bandsmen stood
While breeched and kerchiefed partners whirled, and panted
    To choose each other for good.

She told that far-back day when they learnt astounded
    Of the death of the King of France:

Of the Terror; and then of Bonaparte's unbounded
    Ambition and arrogance.

Of how his threats woke warlike preparations
    Along the southern strand,
And how each night brought tremors and trepidations
    Lest morning should see him land.

She said she had often heard the gibbet creaking
    As it swayed in the lightning flash,
Had caught from the neighbouring town a small child's shrieking
    At the cart-tail under the lash. . . .

With cap-framed face and long gaze into the embers –
    We seated around her knees –
She would dwell on such dead themes, not as one who
        remembers,
    But rather as one who sees.

She seemed one left behind of a band gone distant
    So far that no tongue could hail:
Past things retold were to her as things existent,
    Things present but as a tale.

20 May 1902

The Man He Killed

                    'Had he and I but met
                        By some old ancient inn,
                    We should have sat us down to wet
                        Right many a nipperkin!

                    'But ranged as infantry,
                        And staring face to face,
                    I shot at him as he at me,
                        And killed him in his place.

'I shot him dead because –
  Because he was my foe,
Just so: my foe of course he was;
  That's clear enough; although

'He thought he'd 'list, perhaps,
  Off-hand like – just as I –
Was out of work – had sold his traps –
  No other reason why.

'Yes; quaint and curious war is!
  You shoot a fellow down
You'd treat if met where any bar is,
  Or help to half-a-crown.'

1902

Wagtail and Baby

A baby watched a ford, whereto
  A wagtail came for drinking;
A blaring bull went wading through,
  The wagtail showed no shrinking.

A stallion splashed his way across,
  The birdie nearly sinking;
He gave his plumes a twitch and toss,
  And held his own unblinking.

Next saw the baby round the spot
  A mongrel slowly slinking;
The wagtail gazed, but faltered not
  In dip and sip and prinking.

A perfect gentleman then neared;
  The wagtail, in a winking,
With terror rose and disappeared;
  The baby fell a-thinking.

Channel Firing*

That night your great guns, unawares,
Shook all our coffins as we lay,
And broke the chancel window-squares,
We thought it was the Judgment-day

And sat upright. While drearisome
Arose the howl of wakened hounds:
The mouse let fall the altar-crumb,
The worms drew back into the mounds,

The glebe cow drooled. Till God called, 'No;
It's gunnery practice out at sea
Just as before you went below;
The world is as it used to be:

'All nations striving strong to make
Red war yet redder. Mad as hatters
They do no more for Christés sake
Than you who are helpless in such matters

'That this is not the judgment-hour
For some of them's a blessed thing,
For if it were they'd have to scour
Hell's floor for so much threatening. . . .

'Ha, ha. It will be warmer when
I blow the trumpet (if indeed
I ever do; for you are men,
And rest eternal sorely need).'

So down we lay again. 'I wonder,
Will the world ever saner be,'
Said one, 'than when He sent us under
In our indifferent century!'

And many a skeleton shook his head.
'Instead of preaching forty year,'

My neighbour Parson Thirdly said,
'I wish I had stuck to pipes and beer.'

Again the guns disturbed the hour,
Roaring their readiness to avenge,
As far inland as Stourton Tower,
And Camelot, and starlit Stonehenge.

April 1914

The Convergence of the Twain*

(Lines on the loss of the *Titanic*)

I

In a solitude of the sea
Deep from human vanity,
And the Pride of Life that planned her, stilly couches she.

II

Steel chambers, late the pyres
Of her salamandrine fires,
Cold currents thrid, and turn to rhythmic tidal lyres.

III

Over the mirrors meant
To glass the opulent
The sea-worm crawls – grotesque, slimed, dumb, indifferent.

IV

Jewels in joy designed
To ravish the sensuous mind
Lie lightless, all their sparkles bleared and black and blind.

V

Dim moon-faced fishes near
Gaze at the gilded gear
And query: 'What does this vaingloriousness down here?' . . .

VI

Well: while was fashioning
This creature of cleaving wing,
The Immanent Will that stirs and urges everything

VII

Prepared a sinister mate
For her – so gaily great –
A Shape of Ice, for the time far and dissociate.

VIII

And as the smart ship grew
In stature, grace, and hue,
In shadowy silent distance grew the Iceberg too.

IX

Alien they seemed to be:
No mortal eye could see
The intimate welding of their later history,

X

Or sign that they were bent
By paths coincident
On being anon twin halves of one august event,

XI

Till the Spinner of the Years
Said 'Now!' And each one hears,
And consummation comes, and jars two hemispheres.

When I Set Out for Lyonnesse*

(1870)

When I set out for Lyonnesse,
 A hundred miles away,
 The rime was on the spray,
And starlight lit my lonesomeness
When I set out for Lyonnesse
 A hundred miles away.

What would bechance at Lyonnesse
 While I should sojourn there
 No prophet durst declare,
Nor did the wisest wizard guess
What would bechance at Lyonnesse
 While I should sojourn there.

When I came back from Lyonnesse
 With magic in my eyes,
 All marked with mute surmise
My radiance rare and fathomless,
When I came back from Lyonnesse
 With magic in my eyes!

A Thunderstorm in Town

(A Reminiscence: 1893)

She wore a new 'terra-cotta' dress,
And we stayed, because of the pelting storm,
Within the hansom's dry recess,
Though the horse had stopped; yea, motionless
 We sat on, snug and warm.

Then the downpour ceased, to my sharp sad pain,
And the glass that had screened our forms before
Flew up, and out she sprang to her door:
I should have kissed her if the rain
    Had lasted a minute more.

Beyond the Last Lamp*

(Near Tooting Common)

I

While rain, with eve in partnership,
Descended darkly, drip, drip, drip,
Beyond the last lone lamp I passed
    Walking slowly, whispering sadly,
    Two linked loiterers, wan, downcast:
Some heavy thought constrained each face,
And blinded them to time and place.

II

The pair seemed lovers, yet absorbed
In mental scenes no longer orbed
By love's young rays. Each countenance
    As it slowly, as it sadly
    Caught the lamplight's yellow glance,
Held in suspense a misery
At things which had been or might be.

III

When I retrod that watery way
Some hours beyond the droop of day,
Still I found pacing there the twain
    Just as slowly, just as sadly,
    Heedless of the night and rain.
One could but wonder who they were
And what wild woe detained them there.

IV

Though thirty years of blur and blot
Have slid since I beheld that spot,
And saw in curious converse there
 Moving slowly, moving sadly
 That mysterious tragic pair,
Its olden look may linger on –
All but the couple; they have gone.

V

Whither? Who knows, indeed. . . . And yet
To me, when nights are weird and wet,
Without those comrades there at tryst
 Creeping slowly, creeping sadly,
 That lone lane does not exist.
There they seem brooding on their pain,
And will, while such a lane remain.

My Spirit Will Not Haunt the Mound

My spirit will not haunt the mound
 Above my breast,
But travel, memory-possessed,
To where my tremulous being found
 Life largest, best.

My phantom-footed shape will go
 When nightfall grays
Hither and thither along the ways
I and another used to know
 In backward days.

And there you'll find me, if a jot
 You still should care
For me, and for my curious air;
If otherwise, then I shall not,
 For you, be there.

Wessex Heights

(1896)

There are some heights in Wessex, shaped as if by a kindly hand
For thinking, dreaming, dying on, and at crises when I stand,
Say, on Ingpen Beacon eastward, or on Wylls-Neck westwardly,
I seem where I was before my birth, and after death may be.

In the lowlands I have no comrade, not even the lone man's
    friend –
Her who suffereth long and is kind; accepts what he is too weak
    to mend:
Down there they are dubious and askance; there nobody thinks
    as I,
But mind-chains do not clank where one's next neighbour is the
    sky.

In the towns I am tracked by phantoms having weird detective
    ways –
Shadows of beings who fellowed with myself of earlier days:
They hang about at places, and they say harsh heavy things –
Men with a wintry sneer, and women with tart disparagings.
Down there I seem to be false to myself, my simple self that was,
And is not now, and I see him watching, wondering what crass
    cause
Can have merged him into such a strange continuator as this,
Who yet has something in common with himself, my chrysalis.

I cannot go to the great grey Plain; there's a figure against the
    moon,
Nobody sees it but I, and it makes my breast beat out of tune;
I cannot go to the tall-spired town, being barred by the forms
    now passed
For everybody but me, in whose long vision they stand there fast.

There's a ghost at Yell'ham Bottom chiding loud at the fall of the
    night,

There's a ghost in Froom-side Vale, thin-lipped and vague, in a
    shroud of white,
There is one in the railway train whenever I do not want it near,
I see its profile against the pane, saying what I would not hear.

As for one rare fair woman, I am now but a thought of hers,
I enter her mind and another thought succeeds me that she
    prefers;
Yet my love for her in its fulness she herself even did not know;
Well, time cures hearts of tenderness, and now I can let her go.

So I am found on Ingpen Beacon, or on Wylls-Neck to the west,
Or else on homely Bulbarrow, or little Pilsdon Crest,
Where men have never cared to haunt, nor women have walked
    with me,
And ghosts then keep their distance; and I know some liberty.

Under the Waterfall*

'Whenever I plunge my arm, like this,
In a basin of water, I never miss
The sweet sharp sense of a fugitive day
Fetched back from its thickening shroud of gray.
      Hence the only prime
      And real love-rhyme
      That I know by heart,
      And that leaves no smart,
Is the purl of a little valley fall
About three spans wide and two spans tall
Over a table of solid rock,
And into a scoop of the self-same block;
The purl of a runlet that never ceases
In stir of kingdoms, in wars, in peaces;
With a hollow boiling voice it speaks
And has spoken since hills were turfless peaks.'

'And why gives this the only prime
Idea to you of a real love-rhyme?
And why does plunging your arm in a bowl
Full of spring water, bring throbs to your soul?'
'Well, under the fall, in a crease of the stone,
Though where precisely none ever has known,
Jammed darkly, nothing to show how prized,
And by now with its smoothness opalized,
     Is a drinking-glass:
     For, down that pass
     My lover and I
     Walked under a sky
Of blue with a leaf-wove awning of green,
In the burn of August, to paint the scene,
And we placed our basket of fruit and wine
By the runlet's rim, where we sat to dine;
And when we had drunk from the glass together,
Arched by the oak-copse from the weather,
I held the vessel to rinse in the fall,
Where it slipped, and sank, and was past recall,
Though we stooped and plumbed the little abyss
With long bared arms. There the glass still is.
And, as said, if I thrust my arm below
Cold water in basin or bowl, a throe
From the past awakens a sense of that time,
And the glass we used, and the cascade's rhyme.
The basin seems the pool, and its edge
The hard smooth face of the brook-side ledge,
And the leafy pattern of china-ware
The hanging plants that were bathing there.

'By night, by day, when it shines or lours,
There lies intact that chalice of ours,
And its presence adds to the rhyme of love
Persistently sung by the fall above.
No lip has touched it since his and mine
In turns therefrom sipped lovers' wine.'

from **Poems of 1912–13**

Veteris Vestigia Flammae

The Going*

Why did you give no hint that night
That quickly after the morrow's dawn,
And calmly, as if indifferent quite,
You would close your term here, up and be gone
　　Where I could not follow
　　With wing of swallow
To gain one glimpse of you ever anon!

　　Never to bid good-bye,
　　Or lip me the softest call,
Or utter a wish for a word, while I
Saw morning harden upon the wall,
　　Unmoved, unknowing
　　That your great going
Had place that moment, and altered all.

Why do you make me leave the house
And think for a breath it is you I see
At the end of the alley of bending boughs
Where so often at dusk you used to be;
　　Till in darkening dankness
　　The yawning blankness
Of the perspective sickens me!

　　You were she who abode
　　By those red-veined rocks far West,
You were the swan-necked one who rode
Along the beetling Beeny Crest,

And, reining nigh me,
Would muse and eye me,
While Life unrolled us its very best.

Why, then, latterly did we not speak,
Did we not think of those days long dead,
And ere your vanishing strive to seek
That time's renewal? We might have said,
'In this bright spring weather
We'll visit together
Those places that once we visited.'

Well, well! All's past amend,
Unchangeable. It must go.
I seem but a dead man held on end
To sink down soon. . . . O you could not know
That such swift fleeing
No soul foreseeing –
Not even I – would undo me so!

December 1912

Your Last Drive

Here by the moorway you returned,
And saw the borough lights ahead
That lit your face – all undiscerned
To be in a week the face of the dead,
And you told of the charm of that haloed view
That never again would beam on you.

And on your left you passed the spot
Where eight days later you were to lie,
And be spoken of as one who was not;
Beholding it with a heedless eye
As alien from you, though under its tree
You soon would halt everlastingly.

I drove not with you. . . . Yet had I sat
At your side that eve I should not have seen
That the countenance I was glancing at
Had a last-time look in the flickering sheen,
Nor have read the writing upon your face,
'I go hence soon to my resting-place;

'You may miss me then. But I shall not know
How many times you visit me there,
Or what your thoughts are, or if you go
There never at all. And I shall not care.
Should you censure me I shall take no heed,
And even your praises no more shall need.'

True: never you'll know. And you will not mind.
But shall I then slight you because of such?
Dear ghost, in the past did you ever find
The thought 'What profit,' move me much?
Yet abides the fact, indeed, the same, –
You are past love, praise, indifference, blame.

December 1912

The Walk

You did not walk with me
Of late to the hill-top tree
    By the gated ways,
    As in earlier days;
    You were weak and lame,
    So you never came,
And I went alone, and I did not mind,
Not thinking of you as left behind.

I walked up there to-day
Just in the former way;

Surveyed around
The familiar ground
By myself again:
What difference, then?
Only that underlying sense
Of the look of a room on returning thence.

I Found Her Out There

I found her out there
On a slope few see,
That falls westwardly
To the salt-edged air,
Where the ocean breaks
On the purple strand,
And the hurricane shakes
The solid land.

I brought her here,
And have laid her to rest
In a noiseless nest
No sea beats near.
She will never be stirred
In her loamy cell
By the waves long heard
And loved so well.

So she does not sleep
By those haunted heights
The Atlantic smites
And the blind gales sweep,
Whence she often would gaze
At Dundagel's famed head,
While the dipping blaze
Dyed her face fire-red;

And would sigh at the tale
Of sunk Lyonnesse,
As a wind-tugged tress
Flapped her cheek like a flail;
Or listen at whiles
With a thought-bound brow
To the murmuring miles
She is far from now.

Yet her shade, maybe,
Will creep underground
Till it catch the sound
Of that western sea
As it swells and sobs
Where she once domiciled,
And joy in its throbs
With the heart of a child.

Without Ceremony

It was your way, my dear,
To vanish without a word
When callers, friends, or kin
Had left, and I hastened in
To rejoin you, as I inferred.

And when you'd a mind to career
Off anywhere – say to town –
You were all on a sudden gone
Before I had thought thereon,
Or noticed your trunks were down.

So, now that you disappear
For ever in that swift style,
Your meaning seems to me
Just as it used to be:
'Good-bye is not worth while!'

The Voice

Woman much missed, how you call to me, call to me,
Saying that now you are not as you were
When you had changed from the one who was all to me,
But as at first, when our day was fair.

Can it be you that I hear? Let me view you, then,
Standing as when I drew near to the town
Where you would wait for me: yes, as I knew you then,
Even to the original air-blue gown!

Or is it only the breeze, in its listlessness
Travelling across the wet mead to me here,
You being ever dissolved to wan wistlessness,
Heard no more again far or near?

    Thus I; faltering forward,
    Leaves around me falling,
Wind oozing thin through the thorn from norward,
    And the woman calling.

December 1912

A Circular

As 'legal representative'
I read a missive not my own,
On new designs the senders give
    For clothes, in tints as shown.

Here figure blouses, gowns for tea,
And presentation-trains of state,
Charming ball-dresses, millinery,
    Warranted up to date.

And this gay-pictured, spring-time shout
Of Fashion, hails what lady proud?
Her who before last year ebbed out
    Was costumed in a shroud.

After a Journey

Hereto I come to view a voiceless ghost;
   Whither, O whither will its whim now draw me?
Up the cliff, down, till I'm lonely, lost,
   And the unseen waters' ejaculations awe me.
Where you will next be there's no knowing,
   Facing round about me everywhere,
      With your nut-coloured hair,
And gray eyes, and rose-flush coming and going.

Yes: I have re-entered your olden haunts at last;
   Through the years, through the dead scenes I have tracked you;
What have you now found to say of our past –
   Scanned across the dark space wherein I have lacked you?
Summer gave us sweets, but autumn wrought division?
   Things were not lastly as firstly well
      With us twain, you tell?
But all's closed now, despite Time's derision.

I see what you are doing: you are leading me on
   To the spots we knew when we haunted here together,
The waterfall, above which the mist-bow shone
   At the then fair hour in the then fair weather,
And the cave just under, with a voice still so hollow
   That it seems to call out to me from forty years ago,
      When you were all aglow,
And not the thin ghost that I now frailly follow!

Ignorant of what there is flitting here to see,
   The waked birds preen and the seals flop lazily;

Soon you will have, Dear, to vanish from me,
　For the stars close their shutters and the dawn whitens hazily.
Trust me, I mind not, though Life lours,
　　The bringing me here; nay, bring me here again!
　　　　I am just the same as when
Our days were a joy, and our paths through flowers.

Pentargan Bay

Beeny Cliff

March 1870–March 1913

I

O the opal and the sapphire of that wandering western sea,
And the woman riding high above with bright hair flapping
　　free –
The woman whom I loved so, and who loyally loved me.

II

The pale mews plained below us, and the waves seemed far away
In a nether sky, engrossed in saying their ceaseless babbling say,
As we laughed light-heartedly aloft on that clear-sunned March
　　day.

III

A little cloud then cloaked us, and there flew an irised rain,
And the Atlantic dyed its levels with a dull misfeatured stain,
And then the sun burst out again, and purples prinked the main.

IV

– Still in all its chasmal beauty bulks old Beeny to the sky,
And shall she and I not go there once again now March is nigh,
And the sweet things said in that March say anew there by and by?

V

What if still in chasmal beauty looms that wild weird western
　　shore,

The woman now is – elsewhere – whom the ambling pony bore,
And nor knows nor cares for Beeny, and will laugh there
    nevermore.

At Castle Boterel

As I drive to the junction of lane and highway,
    And the drizzle bedrenches the waggonette,
I look behind at the fading byway,
    And see on its slope, now glistening wet,
        Distinctly yet

Myself and a girlish form benighted
    In dry March weather. We climb the road
Beside a chaise. We had just alighted
    To ease the sturdy pony's load
        When he sighed and slowed.

What we did as we climbed, and what we talked of
    Matters not much, nor to what it led, –
Something that life will not be balked of
    Without rude reason till hope is dead,
        And feeling fled.

It filled but a minute. But was there ever
    A time of such quality, since or before,
In that hill's story? To one mind never,
    Though it has been climbed, foot-swift, foot-sore,
        By thousands more.

Primaeval rocks form the road's steep border,
    And much have they faced there, first and last,
Of the transitory in Earth's long order;
    But what they record in colour and cast
        Is – that we two passed.

And to me, though Time's unflinching rigour,
   In mindless rote, has ruled from sight
The substance now, one phantom figure
   Remains on the slope, as when that night
      Saw us alight.

I look and see it there, shrinking, shrinking,
   I look back at it amid the rain
For the very last time; for my sand is sinking,
   And I shall traverse old love's domain
      Never again.

March 1913

Places

Nobody says: Ah, that is the place
Where chanced, in the hollow of years ago,
What none of the Three Towns cared to know –
The birth of a little girl of grace –
The sweetest the house saw, first or last;
      Yet it was so
      On that day long past.

Nobody thinks: There, there she lay
In a room by the Hoe, like the bud of a flower,
And listened, just after the bedtime hour,
To the hammering chimes that used to play
The quaint Old Hundred-and-Thirteenth tune
      In Saint Andrew's tower
      Night, morn, and noon.

Nobody calls to mind that here
Upon Boterel Hill, where the waggoners skid,
With cheeks whose airy flush outbid
Fresh fruit in bloom, and free of fear,
She cantered down, as if she must fall

(Though she never did),
To the charm of all.

Nay: one there is to whom these things,
That nobody else's mind calls back,
Have a savour that scenes in being lack,
And a presence more than the actual brings;
To whom to-day is beneaped and stale,
  And its urgent clack
  But a vapid tale.

Plymouth, March 1913

Where the Picnic Was

Where we made the fire
In the summer time
Of branch and briar
On the hill to the sea,
I slowly climb
Through winter mire,
And scan and trace
The forsaken place
Quite readily.

Now a cold wind blows,
And the grass is gray,
But the spot still shows
As a burnt circle – aye,
And stick-ends, charred,
Still strew the sward
Whereon I stand,
Last relic of the band
Who came that day!

Yes, I am here
Just as last year,

And the sea breathes brine
From its strange straight line
Up hither, the same
As when we four came.
– But two have wandered far
From this grassy rise
Into urban roar
Where no picnics are,
And one – has shut her eyes
For evermore.

Seen by the Waits

Through snowy woods and shady
   We went to play a tune
To the lonely manor-lady
   By the light of the Christmas moon.

We violed till, upward glancing
   To where a mirror leaned,
It showed her airily dancing,
   Deeming her movements screened;

Dancing alone in the room there,
   Thin-draped in her robe of night;
Her postures, glassed in the gloom there,
   Were a strange phantasmal sight.

She had learnt (we heard when homing)
   That her roving spouse was dead:
Why she had danced in the gloaming
   We thought, but never said.

from **Satires of Circumstance in Fifteen Glimpses**

(First published April 1911)

ii. In Church

'And now to God the Father,' he ends,
And his voice thrills up to the topmost tiles:
Each listener chokes as he bows and bends,
And emotion pervades the crowded aisles.
Then the preacher glides to the vestry-door,
And shuts it, and thinks he is seen no more.

The door swings softly ajar meanwhile,
And a pupil of his in the Bible class,
Who adores him as one without gloss or guile,
Sees her idol stand with a satisfied smile
And re-enact at the vestry-glass
Each pulpit gesture in deft dumb-show
That had moved the congregation so.

xi. In the Restaurant

'But hear. If you stay, and the child be born,
It will pass as your husband's with the rest,
While, if we fly, the teeth of scorn
Will be gleaming at us from east to west;

And the child will come as a life despised;
I feel an elopement is ill-advised!'

'O you realize not what it is, my dear,
To a woman! Daily and hourly alarms
Lest the truth should out. How can I stay here
And nightly take him into my arms!
Come to the child no name or fame,
Let us go, and face it, and bear the shame.'

xii. At the Draper's

'I stood at the back of the shop, my dear,
    But you did not perceive me.
Well, when they deliver what you were shown
    I shall know nothing of it, believe me!'

And he coughed and coughed as she paled and said,
    'O, I didn't see you come in there –
Why couldn't you speak?' – 'Well, I didn't. I left
    That you should not notice I'd been there.

'You were viewing some lovely things. "*Soon required
    For a widow, of latest fashion*;"
And I knew 'twould upset you to meet the man
    Who had to be cold and ashen

'And screwed in a box before they could dress you
    "*In the last new note in mourning*,"
As they defined it. So, not to distress you,
    I left you to your adorning.'

We Sat at the Window

(Bournemouth, 1875)

We sat at the window looking out,
And the rain came down like silken strings
That Swithin's day. Each gutter and spout
Babbled unchecked in the busy way
    Of witless things:
Nothing to read, nothing to see
Seemed in that room for her and me
    On Swithin's day.

We were irked by the scene, by our own selves; yes,
For I did not know, nor did she infer
How much there was to read and guess
By her in me, and to see and crown
    By me in her.
Wasted were two souls in their prime,
And great was the waste, that July time
    When the rain came down.

Afternoon Service at Mellstock

(Circa 1850)

On afternoons of drowsy calm
    We stood in the panelled pew,
Singing one-voiced a Tate-and-Brady psalm
    To the tune of 'Cambridge New'.

We watched the elms, we watched the rooks,
    The clouds upon the breeze,
Between the whiles of glancing at our books,
    And swaying like the trees.

So mindless were those outpourings! –
Though I am not aware
That I have gained by subtle thought on things
Since we stood psalming there.

Heredity

I am the family face;
Flesh perishes, I live on,
Projecting trait and trace
Through time to times anon,
And leaping from place to place
Over oblivion.

The years-heired feature that can
In curve and voice and eye
Despise the human span
Of durance – that is I;
The eternal thing in man,
That heeds no call to die.

On a Midsummer Eve

I idly cut a parsley stalk,
And blew therein towards the moon;
I had not thought what ghosts would walk
With shivering footsteps to my tune.

I went, and knelt, and scooped my hand
As if to drink, into the brook,
And a faint figure seemed to stand
Above me, with the bygone look.

I lipped rough rhymes of chance, not choice,
I thought not what my words might be;
There came into my ear a voice
That turned a tenderer verse for me.

The Blinded Bird

So zestfully canst thou sing?
And all this indignity,
With God's consent, on thee!
Blinded ere yet a-wing
By the red-hot needle thou,
I stand and wonder how
So zestfully thou canst sing!

Resenting not such wrong,
Thy grievous pain forgot,
Eternal dark thy lot,
Groping thy whole life long,
After that stab of fire;
Enjailed in pitiless wire;
Resenting not such wrong!

Who hath charity? This bird.
Who suffereth long and is kind,
Is not provoked, though blind
And alive ensepulchred?
Who hopeth, endureth all things?
Who thinketh no evil, but sings?
Who is divine? This bird.

Lines

To a Movement in Mozart's E-Flat Symphony

Show me again the time
When in the Junetide's prime
We flew by meads and mountains northerly! –
Yea, to such freshness, fairness, fulness, fineness, freeness,
   Love lures life on.

Show me again the day
When from the sandy bay
We looked together upon the pestered sea! –
Yea, to such surging, swaying, sighing, swelling, shrinking,
   Love lures life on.

Show me again the hour
When by the pinnacled tower
We eyed each other and feared futurity! –
Yea, to such bodings, broodings, beatings, blanchings, blessings,
   Love lures life on.

Show me again just this:
The moment of that kiss
Away from the prancing folk, by the strawberry-tree! –
Yea, to such rashness, ratheness, rareness, ripeness, richness,
   Love lures life on.

Begun November 1898

The Oxen

Christmas Eve, and twelve of the clock.
   'Now they are all on their knees,'
An elder said as we sat in a flock
   By the embers in hearthside ease.

We pictured the meek mild creatures where
    They dwelt in their strawy pen,
Nor did it occur to one of us there
    To doubt they were kneeling then.

So fair a fancy few would weave
    In these years! Yet, I feel,
If someone said on Christmas Eve,
    'Come; see the oxen kneel

'In the lonely barton by yonder coomb
    Our childhood used to know,'
I should go with him in the gloom,
    Hoping it might be so.

1915

The Photograph

The flame crept up the portrait line by line
As it lay on the coals in the silence of night's profound,
    And over the arm's incline,
And along the marge of the silkwork superfine,
And gnawed at the delicate bosom's defenceless round.

Then I vented a cry of hurt, and averted my eyes;
The spectacle was one that I could not bear,
    To my deep and sad surprise;
But, compelled to heed, I again looked furtivewise
Till the flame had eaten her breasts, and mouth, and hair.

'Thank God, she is out of it now?' I said at last,
In a great relief of heart when the thing was done
    That had set my soul aghast,
And nothing was left of the picture unsheathed from the past
But the ashen ghost of the card it had figured on.

She was a woman long hid amid packs of years,
She might have been living or dead; she was lost to my sight,
 And the deed that had nigh drawn tears
Was done in a casual clearance of life's arrears;
But I felt as I had put her to death that night!

– Well; she knew nothing thereof did she survive,
And suffered nothing if numbered among the dead;
 Yet – yet – if on earth alive
Did she feel a smart, and with vague strange anguish strive?
If in heaven, did she smile at me sadly and shake her head?

Transformations

Portion of this yew
Is a man my grandsire knew,
Bosomed here at its foot:
This branch may be his wife,
A ruddy human life
Now turned to a green shoot.

These grasses must be made
Of her who often prayed,
Last century, for repose;
And the fair girl long ago
Whom I often tried to know
May be entering this rose.

So, they are not underground,
But as nerves and veins abound
In the growths of upper air,
And they feel the sun and rain,
And the energy again
That made them what they were!

The Last Signal

(11 October 1886)
A Memory Of William Barnes

Silently I footed by an uphill road
That led from my abode to a spot yew-boughed;
Yellowly the sun sloped low down to westward,
    And dark was the east with cloud.

Then, amid the shadow of that livid sad east,
Where the light was least, and a gate stood wide,
Something flashed the fire of the sun that was facing it,
    Like a brief blaze on that side.

Looking hard and harder I knew what it meant –
That sudden shine sent from the livid east scene;
It meant the west mirrored by the coffin of my friend there,
    Turning to the road from his green,

To take his last journey forth – he who in his prime
Trudged so many a time from that gate athwart the land!
Thus a farewell to me he signalled on his grave-way,
    As with a wave of his hand.

Winterborne-Came Path

Great Things

Sweet cyder is a great thing,
    A great thing to me,
Spinning down to Weymouth town
    By Ridgway thirstily,
And maid and mistress summoning
    Who tend the hostelry:
O cyder is a great thing
    A great thing to me!

The dance it is a great thing,
   A great thing to me,
With candles lit and partners fit
   For night-long revelry;
And going home when day-dawning
   Peeps pale upon the lea:
O dancing is a great thing,
   A great thing to me!

Love is, yea, a great thing,
   A great thing to me!
When, having drawn across the lawn
   In darkness silently,
A figure flits like one a-wing
   Out from the nearest tree;
O love is, yes, a great thing,
   A great thing to me!

Will these be always great things,
   Great things to me? . . .
Let it befall that One will call
   'Soul, I have need of thee;'
What then? Joy-jaunts, impassioned flings,
   Love, and its ecstasy,
Will always have been great things,
   Great things to me!

Old Furniture

I know not how it may be with others
   Who sit amid relics of householdry
That date from the days of their mothers' mothers,
   But well I know how it is with me
     Continually.

I see the hands of the generations
        That owned each shiny familiar thing
In play on its knobs and indentations,
        And with its ancient fashioning
                Still dallying:

Hands behinds hands, growing paler and paler,
        As in a mirror a candle-flame
Shows images of itself, each frailer
        As it recedes, though the eye may frame
                Its shape the same.

On the clock's dull dial a foggy finger,
        Moving to set the minutes right
With tentative touches that lift and linger
        In the wont of a moth on a summer night,
                Creeps to my sight.

On this old viol, too, fingers are dancing –
        As whilom – just over the strings by the nut,
The tip of a bow receding, advancing
        In airy quivers, as if it would cut
                The plaintive gut.

And I see a face by that box for tinder,
        Glowing forth in fits from the dark,
And fading again, as the linten cinder
        Kindles to red at the flinty spark,
                Or goes out stark.

Well, well. It is best to be up and doing,
        The world has no use for one to-day
Who eyes things thus – no aim pursuing!
        He should not continue in this stay,
                But sink away.

Logs on the Hearth*

A Memory of a Sister

The fire advances along the log
   Of the tree we felled,
Which bloomed and bore striped apples by the peck
   Till its last hour of bearing knelled.

The fork that first my hand would reach
   And then my foot
In climbings upward inch by inch, lies now
   Sawn, sapless, darkening with soot.

Where the bark chars is where, one year,
   It was pruned, and bled –
Then overgrew the wound. But now, at last,
   Its growings all have stagnated.

My fellow-climber rises dim
   From her chilly grave –
Just as she was, her foot near mine on the bending limb,
   Laughing, her young brown hand awave.

December 1915

The Five Students*

The sparrow dips in his wheel-rut bath,
   The sun grows passionate-eyed,
And boils the dew to smoke by the paddock-path;
   As strenuously we stride, –
Five of us; dark He, fair He, dark She, fair She, I,
   All beating by.

The air is shaken, the high-road hot,
   Shadowless swoons the day,

The greens are sobered and cattle at rest; but not
    We on our urgent way, —
Four of us; fair She, dark She, fair He, I, are there,
    But one — elsewhere.

Autumn moulds the hard fruit mellow,
    And forward still we press
Through moors, briar-meshed plantations, clay-pits yellow,
    As in the spring hours — yes,
Three of us; fair He, fair She, I, as heretofore,
    But fallen one more.

The last leaf drops: earthworms draw it in
    At night-time noiselessly,
The fingers of birch and beech are skeleton-thin,
    And yet on the beat are we, —
Two of us, fair She, I. But no more left to go
    The track we know.

Icicles tag the church-aisle leads,
    The flag-rope gibbers hoarse,
The home-bound foot-folk wrap their snow-flaked heads,
    Yet I still stalk the course —
One of us . . . Dark and fair He, dark and fair She, gone:
    The rest — anon.

During Wind and Rain

They sing their dearest songs —
He, she, all of them — yea,
Treble and tenor and bass,
    And one to play;
With the candles mooning each face . . .
    Ah, no; the years O!
How the sick leaves reel down in throngs!

They clear the creeping moss –
   Elders and juniors – aye,
Making the pathways neat
    And the garden gay;
And they build a shady seat . . .
    Ah, no; the years, the years;
See, the white storm-birds wing across!

They are blithely breakfasting all –
   Men and maidens – yea,
Under the summer tree,
    With a glimpse of the bay,
While pet fowl come to the knee . . . .
    Ah, no; the years O!
And the rotten rose is ript from the wall.

They change to a high new house,
   He, she, all of them – aye,
Clocks and carpets and chairs
    On the lawn all day,
And brightest things that are theirs . . . .
    Ah, no; the years, the years;
Down their carved names the rain-drop ploughs.

It Never Looks Like Summer*

'It never looks like summer here
   On Beeny by the sea.'
But though she saw its looks as drear,
   Summer it seemed to me.

It never looks like summer now
   Whatever weather's there;
But ah, it cannot anyhow,
   On Beeny or elsewhere!

Boscastle
8 March 1913

He Revisits His First School*

I should not have shown in the flesh,
I ought to have gone as a ghost;
It was awkward, unseemly almost,
Standing solidly there as when fresh,
      Pink, tiny, crisp-curled,
      My pinions yet furled
      From the winds of the world.

After waiting so many a year
To wait longer, and go as a sprite
From the tomb at the mid of some night
Was the right, radiant way to appear;
      Not as one wanzing weak
      From life's roar and reek,
      His rest still to seek:

Yea, beglimpsed through the quaint quarried glass
Of green moonlight, by me greener made,
When they'd cry, perhaps, 'There sits his shade
In his olden haunt – just as he was
      When in Walkingame he
      Conned the grand Rule-of-Three
      With the bent of a bee.'

But to show in the afternoon sun,
WIth an aspect of hollow-eyed care,
When none wished to see me come there,
Was a garish thing, better undone.
      Yes; wrong was the way;
      But yet, let me say,
      I may right it – some day.

Midnight on the Great Western*

In the third-class seat sat the journeying boy,
      And the roof-lamp's oily flame
Played down on his listless form and face,
Bewrapt past knowing to what he was going,
      Or whence he came.

In the band of his hat the journeying boy
      Had a ticket stuck; and a string
Around his neck bore the key of his box,
That twinkled gleams of the lamp's sad beams
      Like a living thing.

What past can be yours, O journeying boy
      Towards a world unknown.
Who calmly, as if incurious quite
On all at stake, can undertake
      This plunge alone?

Knows your soul a sphere, O journeying boy,
      Our rude realms far above,
Whence with spacious vision you mark and mete
This region of sin that you find you in,
      But are not of?

The Shadow on the Stone

      I went by the Druid stone
    That broods in the garden white and lone,
  And I stopped and looked at the shifting shadows
      That at some moments fall thereon
      From the tree hard by with a rhythmic swing,
      And they shaped in my imagining
  To the shade that a well-known head and shoulders
      Threw there when she was gardening.

I thought her behind my back,
Yea, her I long had learned to lack,
And I said: 'I am sure you are standing behind me,
    Though how do you get into this old track?'
    And there was no sound but the fall of a leaf
    As a sad response; and to keep down grief
I would not turn my head to discover
    That there was nothing in my belief.

Yet I wanted to look and see
That nobody stood at the back of me;
But I thought once more: 'Nay, I'll not unvision
    A shape which, somehow, there may be.'
    So I went on softly from the glade,
    And left her behind me throwing her shade,
As she were indeed an apparition –
    My head unturned lest my dream should fade.

Begun 1913: finished 1916

In Time of 'The Breaking of Nations'*

I

Only a man harrowing clods
    In a slow silent walk
With an old horse that stumbles and nods
    Half asleep as they stalk.

II

Only thin smoke without flame
    From the heaps of couch-grass;
Yet this will go onward the same
    Though Dynasties pass.

III
Yonder a maid and her wight
    Come whispering by:
War's annals will cloud into night
    Ere their story die

1915

Afterwards

When the Present has latched its postern behind my tremulous
        stay,
    And the May month flaps its glad green leaves like wings,
Delicate-filmed as new-spun silk, will the neighbours say,
    'He was a man who used to notice such things'?

If it be in the dusk when, like an eyelid's soundless blink,
    The dewfall-hawk comes crossing the shades to alight
Upon the wind-warped upland thorn, a gazer may think,
    'To him this must have been a familiar sight.'

If I pass during some nocturnal blackness, mothy and warm,
    When the hedgehog travels furtively over the lawn,
One may say, 'He strove that such innocent creatures should come
        to no harm,
    But he could do little for them; and now he is gone.'

If, when hearing that I have been stilled at last, they stand at the
        door,
    Watching the full-starred heavens that winter sees,
Will this thought rise on those who will meet my face no more,
    'He was one who had an eye for such mysteries'?

And will any say when my bell of quittance is heard in the gloom,
    And a crossing breeze cuts a pause in its outrollings,
Till they rise again, as they were a new bell's boom,
    'He hears it not now, but used to notice such things'?

Weathers

I

This is the weather the cuckoo likes,
          And so do I;
When showers betumble the chestnut spikes,
          And nestlings fly:
And the little brown nightingale bills his best,
And they sit outside at 'The Travellers' Rest',
And maids come forth sprig-muslin drest,
And citizens dream of the south and west,
          And so do I.

II

This is the weather the shepherd shuns,
          And so do I;
When beeches drip in browns and duns,
          And thresh, and ply;
And hill-hid tides throb, throe on throe,
And meadow rivulets overflow,
And drops on gate-bars hang in a row,
And rooks in families homeward go,
          And so do I.

Faintheart in a Railway Train

At nine in the morning there passed a church,
At ten there passed me by the sea,
At twelve a town of smoke and smirch,
At two a forest of oak and birch,
     And then, on a platform, she:

A radiant stranger, who saw not me.
I said, 'Get out to her do I dare?'
But I kept my seat in my search for a plea,

And the wheels moved on. O could it but be
That I had alighted there!

A Man Was Drawing Near to Me*

On that gray night of mournful drone,
Apart from aught to hear, to see,
I dreamt not that from shires unknown
        In gloom, alone,
        By Halworthy,
A man was drawing near to me.

I'd no concern at anything,
No sense of coming pull-heart play;
Yet, under the silent outspreading
        Of even's wing
        Where Otterham lay,
A man was riding up my way.

I thought of nobody – not of one,
But only of trifles – legends, ghosts –
Though, on the moorland dim and dun
        That travellers shun
        About these coasts,
The man had passed Tresparret Posts.

There was no light at all inland,
Only the seaward pharos-fire,
Nothing to let me understand
        That hard at hand
        By Hennett Byre
The man was getting nigh and nigher.

There was a rumble at the door,
A draught disturbed the drapery,
And but a minute passed before,

With gaze that bore
My destiny,
The man revealed himself to me.

The Selfsame Song

A bird sings the selfsame song,
With never a fault in its flow,
That we listened to here those long
        Long years ago.

A pleasing marvel is how
A strain of such rapturous rote
Should have gone on thus till now
        Unchanged in a note!

– But it's not the selfsame bird. –
No: perished to dust is he. . . .
As also are those who heard
        That song with me.

At the Railway Station, Upway

'There is not much that I can do,
    For I've no money that's quite my own!'
    Spoke up the pitying child –
A little boy with a violin
At the station before the train came in, –
'But I can play my fiddle to you,
And a nice one 'tis, and good in tone!'

The man in the handcuffs smiled;
The constable looked, and he smiled, too,

As the fiddle began to twang;
And the man in the handcuffs suddenly sang
　　　With grimful glee:
　　　'This life so free
　　　Is the thing for me!'
And the constable smiled, and said no word,
As if unconscious of what he heard;
And so they went on till the train came in –
The convict, and boy with the violin.

Voices from Things Growing in a Churchyard

These flowers are I, poor Fanny Hurd,
　　　Sir or Madam,
A little girl here sepultured.
Once I flit-fluttered like a bird
Above the grass, as now I wave
In daisy shapes above my grave,
　　　All day cheerily,
　　　All night eerily!

– I am one Bachelor Bowring, 'Gent',
　　　Sir or Madam;
In shingled oak my bones were pent;
Hence more than a hundred years I spent
In my feat of change from a coffin-thrall
To a dancer in green as leaves on a wall,
　　　All day cheerily,
　　　All night eerily!

– I, these berries of juice and gloss,
　　　Sir or Madam,
Am clean forgotten as Thomas Voss;
Thin-urned, I have burrowed away from the moss
That covers my sod, and have entered this yew,

And turned to clusters ruddy of view,
          All day cheerily,
          All night eerily!

– The Lady Gertrude, proud, high-bred,
          Sir or Madam,
Am I – this laurel that shades your head;
Into its veins I have stilly sped,
And made them of me; and my leaves now shine,
As did my satins superfine,
          All day cheerily,
          All night eerily!

– I, who as innocent withwind climb,
          Sir or Madam,
Am one Eve Greensleeves, in olden time
Kissed by men from many a clime,
Beneath sun, stars, in blaze, in breeze,
As now by glowworms and by bees,
          All day cheerily,
          All night eerily!

– I'm old Squire Audeley Grey, who grew,
          Sir or Madam,
Aweary of life, and in scorn withdrew;
Till anon I clambered up anew
As ivy-green, when my ache was stayed,
And in that attire I have longtime gayed
          All day cheerily,
          All night eerily!

– And so these maskers breathe to each
          Sir or Madam
Who lingers there, and their lively speech
Affords an interpreter much to teach,
As their murmurous accents seem to come
Thence hitheraround in a radiant hum,
          All day cheerily,
          All night eerily!

The Children and Sir Nameless

Sir Nameless, once of Athelhall, declared:
'These wretched children romping in my park
Trample the herbage till the soil is bared,
And yap and yell from early morn till dark!
Go keep them harnessed to their set routines:
Thank God I've none to hasten my decay;
For green remembrance there are better means
Than offspring, who but wish their sires away.'

Sir Nameless of that mansion said anon:
'To be perpetuate for my mightiness
Sculpture must image me when I am gone.'
– He forthwith summoned carvers there express
To shape a figure stretching seven-odd feet
(For he was tall) in alabaster stone,
With shield, and crest, and casque, and sword complete:
When done a statelier work has never known.

Three hundred years hied; Church-restorers came,
And, no one of his lineage being traced,
They thought an effigy so large in frame
Best fitted for the floor. There it was placed,
Under the seats for schoolchildren. And they
Kicked out his name, and hobnailed off his nose;
And, as they yawned through sermon-time, they say,
'Who was this old stone man beneath our toes?'

After a Romantic Day

The railway bore him through
An earthen cutting out from a city:
There was no scope for view,

Though the frail light shed by a slim young moon
    Fell like a friendly tune.

    Fell like a liquid ditty,
And the blank lack of any charm
    Of landscape did no harm.
The bald steep cutting, rigid, rough,
    And moon-lit, was enough
For poetry of place: its weathered face
Formed a convenient sheet whereon
The visions of his mind were drawn.

An Ancient to Ancients

Where once we danced, where once we sang,
    Gentlemen,
The floors are sunken, cobwebs hang,
And cracks creep; worms have fed upon
The doors. Yea, sprightlier times were then
Than now, with harps and tabrets gone,
    Gentlemen!

Where once we rowed, where once we sailed,
    Gentlemen,
And damsels took the tiller, veiled
Against too strong a stare (God wot
Their fancy, then or anywhen!)
Upon that shore we are clean forgot,
    Gentlemen!

We have lost somewhat, afar and near,
    Gentlemen,
The thinning of our ranks each year
Affords a hint we are nigh undone,
That we shall not be ever again
The marked of many, loved of one,
    Gentlemen.

In dance the polka hit our wish,
>   Gentlemen,
The paced quadrille, the spry schottische,
'Sir Roger'. – And in opera spheres
The 'Girl' (the famed 'Bohemian'),
And 'Trovatore', held the ears,
>   Gentlemen.

This season's paintings do not please,
>   Gentlemen,
Like Etty, Mulready, Maclise;
Throbbing romance has waned and wanned;
No wizard wields the witching pen
Of Bulwer, Scott, Dumas, and Sand,
>   Gentlemen.

The bower we shrined to Tennyson,
>   Gentlemen,
Is roof-wrecked; damps there drip upon
Sagged seats, the creeper-nails are rust,
The spider is sole denizen;
Even she who voiced those rhymes is dust,
>   Gentlemen!

We who met sunrise sanguine-souled,
>   Gentlemen,
Are wearing weary. We are old;
These younger press; we feel our rout
Is imminent to Aïdes' den, –
That evening shades are stretching out,
>   Gentlemen!

And yet, though ours be failing frames,
>   Gentlemen,
So were some others' history names,
Who trode their track light-limbed and fast
As these youth, and not alien
From enterprise, to their long last,
>   Gentlemen.

Sophocles, Plato, Socrates,
    Gentlemen,
Pythagoras, Thucydides,
Herodotus, and Homer, – yea,
Clement, Augustin, Origen,
Burnt brightlier towards their setting-day,
    Gentlemen.

And ye, red-lipped and smooth-browned; list,
    Gentlemen;
Much is there waits you we have missed;
Much lore we leave you worth the knowing,
Much, much has lain outside our ken:
Nay, rush not: time serves: we are going,
    Gentlemen.

Any little Old Song

Any little old song
    Will do for me,
Tell it of joys gone long,
    Or joys to be,
Or friendly faces best
    Loved to see.

Newest themes I want not
    On subtle strings,
And for thrillings pant not
    That new song brings:
I only need the homeliest
    Of heartstirrings.

In a Former Resort after Many Years

Do I know these, slack-shaped and wan,
Whose substance, one time fresh and furrowless,
Is now a rag drawn over a skeleton,
   As in El Greco's canvasses? –
Whose cheeks have slipped down, lips become indrawn,
   And statures shrunk to dwarfishness?

Do they know me, whose former mind
Was like an open plain where no foot falls,
But now is as a gallery portrait-lined,
   And scored with necrologic scrawls,
Where feeble voices rise, once full-defined,
   From underground in curious calls?

Snow in the Suburbs

    Every branch big with it,
     Bent every twig with it;
    Every fork like a white web-foot;
    Every street and pavement mute:
Some flakes have lost their way, and grope back upward, when
Meeting those meandering down they turn and descend again.
   The palings are glued together like a wall,
   And there is no waft of wind with the fleecy fall.

    A sparrow enters the tree,
     Whereon immediately
    A snow-lump thrice his own slight size
    Descends on him and showers his head and eyes,
      And overturns him,
      And near inurns him,
     And lights on a nether twig, when its brush
Starts off a volley of other lodging lumps with a rush.

The steps are a blanched slope,
Up which, with feeble hope,
A black cat comes, wide-eyed and thin;
And we take him in.

The Frozen Greenhouse

(St Juliot)

'There was a frost
Last night!' she said,
'And the stove was forgot
When we went to bed,
And the greenhouse plants
Are frozen dead!'

By the breakfast blaze
Blank-faced spoke she,
Her scared young look
Seeming to be
The very symbol
Of tragedy.

The frost is fiercer
Than then to-day,
As I pass the place
Of her once dismay,
But the greenhouse stands
Warm, tight, and gay,

While she who grieved
At the sad lot
Of her pretty plants –
Cold, iced, forgot –
Herself is colder,
And knows it not.

Nobody Comes*

Tree-leaves labour up and down,
    And through them the fainting light
    Succumbs to the crawl of night.
Outside in the road the telegraph wire
    To the town from the darkening land
Intones to travellers like a spectral lyre
    Swept by a spectral hand.

A car comes up, with lamps full-glare,
    That flash upon a tree:
    It has nothing to do with me,
And whangs along in a world of its own,
    Leaving a blacker air;
And mute by the gate I stand again alone,
    And nobody pulls up there.

9 October 1924

Shortening Days at the Homestead

The first fire since the summer is lit, and is smoking into the room:
    The sun-rays thread it through, like woof-lines in a loom.
    Sparrows spurt from the hedge, whom misgivings appal
That winter did not leave last year for ever, after all.
    Like shock-headed urchins, spiny-haired,
    Stand pollard willows, their twigs just bared.

Who is this coming with pondering pace,
    Black and ruddy, with white embossed,
His eyes being black, and ruddy his face,
And the marge of his hair like morning frost?
      It's the cider-maker,
      And appletree-shaker,
And behind him on wheels, in readiness,
His mill, and tubs, and vat, and press.

Proud Songsters

The thrushes sing as the sun is going,
And the finches whistle in ones and pairs,
And as it gets dark loud nightingales
      In bushes
Pipe, as they can when April wears,
    As if all Time were theirs.

These are brand-new birds of twelve-months' growing,
Which a year ago, or less than twain,
No finches were, nor nightingales,
      Nor thrushes,
But only particles of grain,
    And earth, and air, and rain.

A Wish for Unconsciousness

If I could but abide
As a tablet on a wall,
Or a hillock daisy-pied,
Or a picture in a hall,
And as nothing else at all,
I should feel no doleful achings,
I should hear no judgment-call,
Have no evil dreams or wakings,
No uncouth or grisly care;
In a word, no cross to bear.

To Louisa in the Lane*

Meet me again as at that time
   In the hollow of the lane;
I will not pass as in my prime
   I passed at each day's wane.
     – Ah, I remember!
To do it you will have to see
Anew this sorry scene wherein you have ceased to be!

But I will welcome your aspen form
   As you gaze wondering round
And say with spectral frail alarm,
   'Why am I still here found?
     – Ah, I remember!
It is through him with blitheful brow
Who did not love me then, but loves and draws me now!'

And I shall answer: 'Sweet of eyes,
   Carry me with you, Dear,
To where you donned this spirit-guise;
   It's better there than here!'
     – Till I remember
Such is a deed you cannot do:
Wait must I, till with flung-off flesh I follow you.

The Lodging-House Fuchsias

Mrs Masters's fuchsias hung
Higher and broader, and brightly swung,
   Bell-like, more and more
Over the narrow garden-path,
Giving the passer a sprinkle-bath
   In the morning.

She put up with their pushful ways,
And made us tenderly lift their sprays,
    Going to her door:
But when her funeral had to pass
They cut back all the flowery mass
    In the morning.

Throwing a Tree

New Forest

The two executioners walk along over the knolls,
Bearing two axes with heavy heads shining and wide,
And a long limp two-handled saw toothed for cutting great
    boles,
And so they approach the proud tree that bears the death-mark on
    its side.

Jackets doffed they swing axes and chop away just above
    ground,
And the chips fly about and lie white on the moss and fallen
    leaves;
Till a broad deep gash in the bark is hewn all the way round,
And one of them tries to hook upward a rope, which at last he
    achieves.

The saw then begins, till the top of the tall giant shivers:
The shivers are seen to grow greater each cut than before:
They edge out the saw, tug the rope; but the tree only quivers,
And kneeling and sawing again, they step back to try pulling once
    more.

Then, lastly, the living mast sways, further sways: with a
    shout
Job and Ike rush aside. Reached the end of its long staying
    powers

The tree crashes downward: it shakes all its neighbours
    throughout,
And two hundred years' steady growth has been ended in less than
    two hours.

Childhood among the Ferns*

I sat one sprinkling day upon the lea,
Where tall-stemmed ferns spread out luxuriantly,
And nothing but those tall ferns sheltered me.

The rain gained strength, and damped each lopping frond,
Ran down their stalks beside me and beyond,
And shaped slow-creeping rivulets as I conned,

With pride, my spray-roofed house. And though anon
Some drops pierced its green rafters, I sat on,
Making pretence I was not rained upon.

The sun then burst, and brought forth a sweet breath
From the limp ferns as they dried underneath:
I said: 'I could live on here thus till death;'

And queried in the green rays as I sate:
'Why should I have to grow to man's estate,
And this afar-noised World perambulate?'

We Field-Women

How it rained
When we worked at Flintcomb-Ash,
And could not stand upon the hill
Trimming swedes for the slicing-mill.
The wet washed through us – plash, plash, plash:
How it rained!

How it snowed
When we crossed from Flintcomb-Ash
To the Great Barn for drawing reed,
Since we could nowise chop a swede. –
Flakes in each doorway and casement-sash:
How it snowed!

How it shone
When we went from Flintcomb-Ash
To start at dairywork once more
In the laughing meads, with cows three-score,
And pails, and songs, and love – too rash:
How it shone!

He Never Expected Much

[or]
A Consideration
[A reflection] on My Eighty-Sixth Birthday

Well, World, you have kept faith with me,
Kept faith with me;
Upon the whole you have proved to be
Much as you said you were.
Since as a child I used to lie
Upon the leaze and watch the sky,

Never, I own, expected I
　　　That life would all be fair.

'Twas then you said, and since have said,
　　　Times since have said,
In that mysterious voice you shed
　　　From clouds and hills around:
'Many have loved me desperately,
Many with smooth serenity,
While some have shown contempt of me
　　　Till they dropped underground.

'I do not promise overmuch,
　　　　Child; overmuch;
Just neutral-tinted haps and such,'
　　　You said to minds like mine.
Wise warning for your credit's sake!
Which I for one failed not to take,
And hence could stem such strain and ache
　　　As each year might assign.

A Necessitarian's Epitaph

A world I did not wish to enter
Took me and poised me on my centre,
Made me grimace, and foot, and prance,
As cats on hot bricks have to dance
Strange jigs to keep them from the floor,
Till they sink down and feel no more.

The Third Kissing-Gate

She foots it forward down the town,
  Then leaves the lamps behind,
And trots along the eastern road
  Where elms stand double-lined.

She clacks the first dim kissing-gate
  Beneath the storm-strained trees,
And passes to the second mead
  That fringes Mellstock Leaze.

She swings the second kissing-gate
  Next the gray garden-wall,
And sees the third mead stretching down
  Towards the waterfall.

And now the third-placed kissing-gate
  Her silent shadow nears,
And touches with; when suddenly
  Her person disappears.

What chanced by that third kissing-gate
  When the hushed mead grew dun?
Lo - two dark figures clasped and closed
  As if they werc but one.

Christmas: 1924

'Peace upon earth!' was said. We sing it,
And pay a million priests to bring it.
After two thousand years of mass
We've got as far as poison-gas.

1924

Dead 'Wessex' the Dog to the Household*

Do you think of me at all,
    Wistful ones?
Do you think of me at all
    As if nigh?
Do you think of me at all
At the creep of evenfall,
Or when the sky-birds call
    As they fly?

Do you look for me at times,
    Wistful ones?
Do you look for me at times,
    Strained and still?
Do you look for me at times,
When the hour for walking chimes,
On that grassy path that climbs
    Up the hill?

You may hear a jump or trot,
    Wistful ones,
You may hear a jump or trot –
    Mine, as 'twere –
You may hear a jump or trot
On the stair or path or plot;
But I shall cause it not,
    Be not there.

Should you call as when I knew you,
    Wistful ones,
Should you call as when I knew you,
    Shared your home;
Should you call as when I knew you,
I shall not turn to view you,
I shall not listen to you,
    Shall not come.

A Private Man on Public Men

When my contemporaries were driving
Their coach through Life with strain and striving,
And raking riches into heaps,
And ably pleading in the Courts
With smart rejoinders and retorts,
Or where the Senate nightly keeps
Its vigils, till their fames were fanned
By rumour's tongue throughout the land,
I lived in quiet, screened, unknown,
Pondering upon some stick or stone,
Or news of some rare book or bird
Latterly bought, or seen, or heard,
Not wishing ever to set eyes on
The surging crowd beyond the horizon,
Tasting years of moderate gladness
Mellowed by sundry days of sadness,
Shut from the noise of the world without,
Hearing but dimly its rush and rout,
Unenvying those amid its roar,
Little endowed, not wanting more.

He Resolves to Say No More

O my soul, keep the rest unknown!
It is too like a sound of moan
          When the charnel-eyed
          Pale Horse has nighed:
Yea, none shall gather what I hide!

Why load men's minds with more to bear
That bear already ails to spare?
          From now alway

Till my last day
What I discern I will not say.

Let Time roll backward if it will;
(Magians who drive the midnight quill
　　With brain aglow
　　Can see it so,)
What I have learnt no man shall know.

And if my vision range beyond
The blinkered sight of souls in bond,
　　– By truth made free –
　　I'll let all be,
And show to no man what I see.

Notes

Hardy published eight volumes of verse, the last of them posthumously: *Wessex Poems* (1898, 51 poems), *Poems of the Past and the Present* (1901, 99 poems), *Time's Laughingstocks* (1909, 94 poems), *Satires of Circumstance* (1914, 107 poems), *Moments of Vision* (1917, 159 poems), *Late Lyrics and Earlier* (1922, 151 poems), *Human Shows* (1925, 152 poems), *Winter Words* (1928, 105 poems). All of these, together with a number of poems and fragments uncollected by Hardy, are included in *The Complete Poems of Thomas Hardy* (1976), edited by James Gibson, on which the text of the present selection is based.

In compiling these notes I have been greatly indebted to Richard Little Purdy's *Thomas Hardy: A Bibliographical Study* (1954) and F. B. Pinion's *A Commentary on the Poems of Thomas Hardy* (1976).

p. 6 *Thoughts of Phena*: 'Phena' is Hardy's cousin Tryphena Sparks (1851–90), with whom he may have had a close relationship in his early years.

p. 8 *In a Eweleaze near Weatherbury*: a eweleaze is as meadow used for grazing sheep; Weatherbury is Hardy's fictional name for Puddletown, near Dorchester.

p. 10 *Drummer Hodge*: As the Afrikaans words in this poem suggest, it was inspired by the Boer War (1899–1902). When the poem was first published in a magazine on 25 November 1899 it was titled 'The Dead Drummer' and the following note was added: 'One of the Drummers killed was a native of a village near Casterbridge.'

p. 11 *Shelley's Skylark*: Shelley, who was Hardy's favourite poet, wrote his poem 'To a Skylark' at Leghorn (Livorno) in Italy in 1820.

p. 13 *To Lizbie Browne*: The subject of this poem was Elizabeth Bishop, the daughter of a local gamekeeper, who 'won Hardy's boyish admiration. But she despised him, as being two or three years her junior . . .' (Hardy, *The Life and Work of Thomas Hardy*, ed. Michael Millgate (1984), p. 30).

p. 15 *A Broken Appointment*: There is evidence that this poem refers to Florence Henniker and the British Museum. Hardy met Mrs Henniker in 1893 and formed a strong but one-sided romantic attachment to her. She is probably also the 'rare fair woman' who is the subject of the penultimate stanza of 'Wessex Heights'.

p. 19 *The Darkling Thrush*: Originally published on 29 December 1900 under the title 'By the Century's Deathbed'.

p. 20 *The Comet at Yell'ham*: Hardy had observed Encke's Comet in 1858.

p. 23 *A Trampwoman's Tragedy*: Hardy wrote this poem, 'a ballad based on some local story of an event more or less resembling the incidents embodied', in April 1902 and was later reported to have regarded it as 'upon the whole, his most successful poem' (*Life and Work*, pp. 335, 517). The manuscript gives the date more precisely as 1827, and according to Hardy the woman's name was Mary Ann Taylor.

p. 26 *A Sunday Morning Tragedy*: Written in January 1904. It was rejected by the *Fortnightly Review* on the grounds that the magazine 'circulated amongst young people' and was eventually printed by Ford Madox Ford in the *English Review.*

p. 35 *A Church Romance*: This poem refers to the courtship of Hardy's parents. Despite the subtitle, they did not in fact marry until 22 December 1839 and Hardy himself was conceived out of wedlock.

p. 36 *After the Last Breath*: Jemima Hardy, the writer's mother, died on 3 April 1904. According to Michael Millgate she was 'the single most important influence in his life' (*Thomas Hardy: A Biography* (1982), p. 435).

p. 37 *One We Knew*: 'M.H.' is Hardy's paternal grandmother, Mary Hardy.

p. 40 *Channel Firing*: Written and published a few months before the outbreak of the First World War.

p. 41 *The Convergence of the Twain*: On 15 April 1912 the S.S. *Titanic* sank, with the loss of 1513 lives, after colliding with an iceberg during her maiden voyage. Hardy was recruited as a member of a subcommittee that organized a 'Dramatiac and Operatic Matinée in Aid of the "Titanic" Disaster Fund', and wrote the poem, later revised and expanded, for recitation as part of a programme at Covent Garden on 24 May 1912.

p. 43 *When I Set Out for Lyonnesse*: On 7 March 1870 Hardy travelled from his home in Dorset to St Juliot in Cornwall on architectural business and there met Emma Gifford, who later became his wife. The episode is recreated from Emma's point of view in 'A Man Was Drawing Near to Me'. Lyonnesse is a traditional name for Cornwall, used in the Arthurian legends told by Malory and revived by Tennyson.

p. 44 *Beyond the Last Lamp*: Hardy and his wife lived in Tooting, a suburb in South London, 1878–81.

p. 47 *Under the Waterfall*: The scene of this incident from Hardy's courtship of Emma Gifford is the Valency valley near St Juliot.

p. 49 *The Going*: This and the eleven poems that follow are selected from the sequence written during the months after Emma's death on 27 November 1912. The Latin epigraph means 'traces of an old fire'.

p. 72 *Logs on the Hearth*: The subject is the poet's much-loved younger sister, Mary Hardy, who died on 24 November 1915.

p. 72 *The Five Students*: Of the individuals referred to, 'dark He' is probably Horace Moule, a close friend who committed suicide in 1873; 'dark She' is Helen Holder, Emma Hardy's sister (died 1900); 'fair She' is Emma herself (died 1912); 'fair He' cannot be identified with confidence.

p. 74 *It Never Looks Like Summer*: Written soon after Emma's death, when Hardy revisited the Cornish scenes of their first meeting and courtship.

p. 75 *He Revisits His First School*: In 1848 Hardy was the first pupil in the newly opened National School at Lower Bockhampton. 'Walkingame' was a standard textbook of arithmetic.

p. 76 *Midnight on the Great Western*: See Part Fifth, Chapter 3 of Hardy's *Jude the Obscure* for a parallel passage.

p. 77 In Time of 'The Breaking of Nations': The quoted phrase in the title is adapted from a passage in the book of Jeremiah in the Old Testament. According to Hardy, the idea for the poem had come to him forty-five years earlier, during the Franco-Prussian War, while visiting St Juliot in Cornwall.

p. 80 A Man Was Drawing Near to Me: See note above on 'When I Set Out for Lyonnesse'.

p. 90 Nobody Comes: This precisely dated poem refers to Florence Hardy's homecoming after a period spent in hospital. She had undergone surgery for cancer on 30 September and returned home on 9 October.

p. 92 To Louisa in the Lane: The poem recalls Hardy's unrequited love, at about the age of sixteen, for a local farmer's daughter, Louisa Harding. She died in 1913, but the poem seems to have been written not long before Hardy's own death in 1928.

p. 94 Childhood among the Ferns: Another poem paralleled in *Jude the Obscure* (see note above on 'Midnight on the Great Western'): cf. the second chapter of that novel and also a strikingly similar passage in Hardy's autobiography (*Life and Work*, p. 20).

p. 98 Dead 'Wessex' the Dog to the Household: A companion of Hardy's later years, 'Wessex' was 'put to sleep' on 27 December 1926.